Praise for *Blackbird Flying*

Nickerson watches and records, searching not only for birds, but also for apparitions and enlightenment, for a deeper understanding of life's twists and turns, its disappointments and betrayals. The shiny bits she collects gleam and shine. The breadth of her attention and knowledge is dazzling.

Geraldine Connolly, poet
Aileron and *Hand of the Wind.*

Seeking the territory of home and love, Nickerson follows historical guides, observes the birds, and explores the shifting nature of memory itself. From the disappearance of the Roanoke colony to string theory to slavery to Louisa May Alcott, the reader is privy to thought-provoking perspectives on life, death, and the importance of truly inhabiting every moment.

Lana Hechtman Ayers, editor, MoonPath Press;
author, *Time Flash; Another Me.*

Sheila Nickerson's book is as comfortable and brisk as wearing an old shirt on a cool day. True, lyrical, and expansive, her essays migrate across subjects that are tangled like the weave of a bird's nest. Birders will love this collection. Readers who can't tell a robin from a raptor will too. Because the bird at the center is the heart we all share.

Christopher Cokinos,
Bodies, of the Holocene: Essays and *The Fallen Sky:
An Intimate History of Shooting Stars.*

Blackbird
Flying

Other works by Sheila Nickerson

Disappearance: A Map

Midnight to the North

Harnessed to the Pole:
Sledge Dogs in Service to American Explorers of the Arctic,
1853-1909

Poetry

Hitchhiking the Highway of Tears
Along the Alaska Highway
In an August Garden
Feast of the Animals: An Alaska Bestiary, Vols 1 and 2
On Why the Quilt-Maker Became a Dragon
Waiting for the News of Death
Songs of the Pine-Wife
To the Waters and the Wild: Poems of Alaska
Letter from Alaska and Other Poems

Blackbird Flying

a memoir

Sheila Nickerson

PUBLISHING

Ashland, Oregon

Book design by Ray Rhamey

ISBN 978-0-9998089-6-2

Library of Congress Control Number: 2018956921

To Martin and All Those Who Travel with Me

But why should we care about angels when
the season's first blackbirds spread
their red-shouldered wings?

Chet Raymo

Watching from the Edge

In the January fog, a Great Egret stands in the tall brown grass against a gray background: an S-shaped rip in the screen that separates us from what is beyond—the pale undying lands. If I were Japanese and writing with brushes, or Russian and writing icons, I would stop here and let Great Egret unfold the story. But I am not. If I were honest, I would admit it is hard to wait for a long-legged bird to deliver the news.

At high tide, when the water floods up the creek that is our part of the river, there are no birds except the short-legged ones on the lawn between our screened-in porch and the sea wall.

These are the birds that interest me: They are blackbirds, common and numerous, the ones we usually look past with our binoculars in order to find the egrets, the ibises, the herons, and ospreys. Their commonness attracts me. If I observe them closely enough, I might learn something—I am not sure what but something, I think, that has to do with ghosts.

Recently, my mother died and now is a ghost. She had lived as a blackbird, a common member of a large flock sharing certain similar characteristics—an Irish Catholic family not long from County Kilkenny, now settled in New York.

As a member of this flock, destined to follow, I needed to know how I might find my way to where she had flown and learn its name. It would be an expedition, but one moving backward as well as forward and offering no assurance of success. Moreover, it would require that I become birder and explorer, hunter and historian, maker of language and tools, cartographer of imagination. And this I could not do alone.

My father was long since gone. At the age of sixty I was left with a younger sister and an estranged older brother. My mother's death shocked me into a new awareness. I was now the oldest woman and the matriarch of my family and, as such, had certain responsibilities. Chief among these was to map a new course and provide navigation for those who followed. Blackbirds are remarkably diverse and flexible and their accomplishments notable. There would be much to consider, but I had to hurry; already news of my mother's death was fading and memories of her life on earth dissolving.

My mother was not an outdoor person; I am quite sure she never went birding. Born and brought up in New York, she was city through and through, though she did attend Bennington College in Vermont as one of its first students. She loved Central Park and was comfortable with the animals of everyday life. She had a fascination with monkeys and liked going to the Central Park Zoo to observe them but never sought them out in a jungle. She took no trips of discovery, though she did venture on trips of pleasure to places such as Europe, Bermuda, Florida, and the Caribbean—all very common for her species and time.

I picture her among Rock Doves, the common feral pigeons, and House Sparrows, the ubiquitous birds of cities introduced from Europe in the mid-1800's, the time of the Irish potato blight, and now considered an invasive species. What she sought, but did not always find, was what these urban species seek: a safe lodging in the midst of crowds, a secure crevice in a busy place. I wished she might have had protection.

She was born at home on Christmas Eve 1915 and, in the morning, put in a box under the tree for her brothers and sister (eventually she would have six siblings) to discover when they dashed for their presents. She was named Mavis, after the Old World songbird (*Turdus philomelos*), a kind of thrush like the American Robin, a bird beautiful in form and song but so common we hardly stop to notice—like the blackbird. She was small, delicate, timid, and had a lovely face.

She enjoyed silly stories and gossip of the rich and famous. Though she was a daily reader of *The New York Times*, she would savor *The New York Post* on weekends to keep up with local scandals.

She loved children and dogs and liked to sit in the park watching people go by, but she lived in darkness also, gripped by alcoholism, the "curse of the Irish," which swept through her family along with different strains of mental illness which were not discussed. Born into a strict Catholic family, she remained a true daughter of the Church—respectful but not enthusiastic.

Much had changed for her. In her youth she lived in wealth. At her New York house, the standing order was that an abundant tea was to be prepared and in readiness every afternoon whether anyone showed up or not.

In later life, after marriage, divorce, three children, addiction, and a long, painful recovery, she lived alone in a small co-op apartment in the Carnegie Hill neighborhood of Manhattan in a building with a doorman named Angel. You might think that gave her special protection, but I must tell you it did not. An angel at the door can do only so much.

The Popularity of Watching Birds

Approximately every five years, the U. S. Fish & Wildlife Service (USFWS) publishes a national survey listing the number of Americans who participate in wildlife-related recreational activities. In 2011, they listed 71.8 million wildlife watchers, 92 percent of whom watch birds.

I was somewhere in this number. Never a serious participant but married to one, I had long been aware of birds, lived consciously among them in Alaska for many years, been on numerous bird walks, and traveled to some of the most bountiful National Wildlife Refuges in the country: Bosque Del Apache, Sacramento, Salton Sea, Merritt Island, Savannah, Parker River, Kern. I had watched birds in Hawaii, Africa, England, Australia, the South Pacific, the Galapagos Islands, and the Caribbean.

I had begun to appreciate not only the beauty of birds but also the beauty of order inherent in their classification. There was satisfaction in identifying and listing them, something akin to the skill of recognizing stars and sailing by celestial navigation.

The history of taxonomy is itself a journey: a long, rich river of exploration which never ends. Swedish naturalist Carl

Linnaeus published his *Species Naturae* 10th Edition in 1758, establishing the system for zoological nomenclature. Although many other travelers on this river had fed into his work and many others would refine it, his was the first atlas, the one that would establish the coordinates and describe the continents of the living kingdoms. Still, it is a river of surprise where the unexpected is always possible and shoals of disagreement abound. Course corrections are constantly needed. New information, such as that streaming from DNA, demands shifts, though shifts in science are hard fought. There is resistance to the unexpected and divergent.

Recently, those who study the brains of birds have been revealing revolutionary news: the cerebrum of a bird, far from simple as was long thought, is similar to that of a mammal and capable of complex behavior. Ravens, it is now known, can use memory to plan for future food retrieval: By remembering past events, such as how they secured a certain food, they can anticipate what will happen at a later time and act accordingly to obtain it.

Crows play and use tools. Experts say the textbook on the avian brain must be rewritten and new terms must be found to discuss the discovery. Dr. Erich D. Jarvis of Duke University, a leader of the Avian Brain Nomenclature Consortium, states: "Old terminology has hindered scientific progress." (*New York Times*, February 1, 2005) The same could be said for cosmology. We simply do not have the words to describe the limitless and mysterious sphere we inhabit. Lacking the vocabulary, we limit our vision and discussion.

The study of birdsong, too, has revealed new complexities. Avian bioacoustics is an algebra built on the symbols of the sonograph. Call by call, line by line, answers emerge to the ancient question of why birds sing. Maybe someday we will more fully know.

In taxonomy, all begins with the mystical number seven: Kingdom, Phylum, Class, Order, Family, Genus, Species. Seven is the number of ritual and fairytale, the number of the continents and seas, the ages of man, the wonders of the ancient world, the deadly sins, the chakras, the days of the week, the spots on a ladybug, the archangels. Classification by sevens holds together and defines what otherwise might be considered a chaos between Heaven and Earth; it helps us to know the niche we inhabit and find comfort in parameters.

But even magic cannot hold back time and discovery. For Linnaeus, there were two kingdoms, Animal and Vegetable. He could not see, or imagine, the many other life forms that existed, whether deep beneath the ocean or too small to notice.

By the twenty-first century, biologists had determined there are five (or, according to some, six) kingdoms with three higher realms termed "domains." Classifications such as "subdivisions," "super families," and "tribes" sprouted, while new possibilities opened more questions. Clearly, taxonomy needs to stretch—and stretch again—towards new visions of relationships and new words to describe them.

All birds belong to the class Aves. The American Ornithological Society maintains the official taxonomic designations with its Check-list of Birds of North and Middle America. But there are numerous other lists, all of which vary as designations and numbers change, and the numbers are large. The family Icteridae alone includes over 100 species worldwide and many thousands of species, fueling the enthusiasm among bird-watchers for chasing down and claiming listing rights to as many of these as possible.

A serious birder might claim 500 for a life list. The indefatigable (and appropriately named) Phoebe Snetsinger of Webster Groves, Missouri, claimed over 8,300 at the time of her death—-during a birding tour in Madagascar in 1999, shortly after she had viewed the extremely rare Red-shouldered Vanga. Her list, exceeding any other by 2,000, will grow posthumously as increasing numbers of subspecies are upgraded to species. It is estimated that the 10,000 species recognized now could swell to 18,000.

Regardless of numbers and length of life lists, there is no "trash" bird. Every one sighted is important. Every one, no matter how common, plays its unique role in the nation of wings.

As with most people, my awareness of birds came slowly. My first pet was a canary, but I do not remember the particulars of how it lived or died. There was a neighbor's tame crow who stole nails and other shiny items from carpenters working on our roof and food from our table and our hands when we ate outside.

Today, I like to think that *aves*, Latin plural for *avis*, is also the plural of *ave*, Latin for "hail, welcome" and also "farewell, goodbye." I like to think that birds greet us and salute us as we make our way across the Earth and accompany us to the hidden worlds beyond.

According to Aristophanes, Eros mated with Chaos and created the birds; thus, they were not only first to see the light but they were also older than all the other gods. Older than gods, pioneers of light—these were the winged beings I would follow.

Blackbird: Order and Family

A blackbird is a member of the Order Passeriformes, the perching birds which are also songbirds. These birds, as apparently diverse as raven and finch, are known not only for their foot structure, which enables them to grip a branch or stalk, but also for the structure of their palate, bill, and wing.

Within this order, the blackbird belongs to the Family Icteridae: various robin-sized birds with pointed bills that migrate and winter together in particularly large flocks. They include Red-winged and Yellow-headed Blackbirds, along with Common Grackles, Brown-headed Cowbirds, Eastern and Western Meadowlarks, and Bobolinks, along with nine species of orioles. In North America, they total 23 species in 8 genera.

A blackbird is not a crow; nor, in spite of its name, is it merely any bird that is black. Rather, it is a bird with its own specific niche in the taxonomic hierarchy.

Further, this bird is not to be confused with the "blackbird" of the Old World, the one that pops up in English nursery rhymes and gothic tales. *That* blackbird (*Turdus merula*) is a species of thrush which breeds in Europe, Asia, and North

Africa and has been introduced to Australia and New Zealand. The national bird of Sweden, it has no evolutionary ties with the icterid family of the New World. The male, all black, is marked by a yellow eye ring and bill, while the juveniles and females are mostly brown. Like many of the icterids, it has a wide range of vocalizations and is known for its melodious song, commemorated deep in our culture by the childhood lyric, "Sing a Song of Six Pence." But, in spite of such cultural ties, this European bird is not our New World blackbird.

With the exception of the Family Fringillidae (Finches and Allies) and the Family Passeridae (Old World Sparrows), blackbirds come at the end of the bird book. They are so far to the back, in fact, they could be overlooked or never reached by an impatient reader hurrying from page to page.

In terms of evolution, Passeriformes Icteridae have succeeded. One reason these smaller birds are so numerous and common is that they have adapted to human-disturbed and human-created environments. They have not only learned to be our neighbor, they have thrived as our neighbor, moving with us as we bulldoze our way across the land. Creatures of the edge, they adapt to new frontiers, pushing along with us as we knock down what is before us. They have found their niche on lawns, parking lots, golf courses, and along beaches and marshes where so many of us have chosen to live in order to have a view of water and what we hope will provide peaceful surroundings. Grackles invade cities, where they have become adept at foraging in Dumpsters and protected areas in spite of deterrents such as noise-making equipment.

It is not unknown for blackbirds to learn to fish, or to pick insects off a car grille in a parking lot. In cities, they have learned to trap, kill, and eat other birds.

After breeding, blackbirds of the northern areas migrate south in huge foraging flocks of mixed species: a curse to farmers and a complaint to those who feed and watch birds. How to get rid of blackbirds is a common question asked politely among birders and less so among farmers. A blackbird "depredation" plan managed by the U.S. Fish & Wildlife Service continues to evolve.

Blackbirds, like all migratory birds, are protected by the Migratory Bird Treaty Act of 1918, a statute which prohibits the pursuit, capture, or killing of over 1,000 migratory species and also protects their feathers, eggs, and nests. The Treaty, in need of updating to meet ecological threats, is administered by USFWS. (All birds except pigeons, House Sparrows, and starlings—along with their nests and eggs—are protected by federal and state laws.)

Every winter thousands of grackles migrate to southern cities which must constantly find new ways to repel them. In Dallas, "startle" devices making use of light and noise have been used, but now natural predators—barn and screech owls—are being called into duty, with programs encouraging residents to set out nesting boxes for them.

Scheduling is particularly important to some species of migrating blackbirds. Male Red-winged Blackbirds leave northern nesting areas after the females and arrive back at the northern nesting sites one to five weeks ahead of the females in order to claim territory that will be attractive to potential mates. Although they do not mate until two years old, they must establish a territory in preparation, for it is the territory that concerns the female. Male Bobolinks also arrive at the nesting grounds before the females; once there, they teach the younger males the local songs to make sure that their dialect survives. But now the Bobolink is under threat since the variegated fields it favors for nesting are being replaced by monochromatic crops cut too quickly for the length of its reproductive cycle.

These pieces of information hold my attention because they remind me of my family in the broadest sense——how they, through the centuries, have had to move and adapt to changing conditions. Ten thousand species of birds now stretch over the world. My people—my mother's people—the Cuddihys and the McGuires, must have spread in comparable numbers. They have survived the Great Irish Potato Famine of 1845-1849, which killed one million and caused another two million to emigrate from Ireland. They have also experienced discrimination and success, alcoholism, political struggles, and war. They have, like birds, found their way through incalculable miles of storm and hunger to bring me here in this moment.

Red-winged Blackbird: Victor

In spite of such competition with farmers, the pressures of climate change, and habitat degradation, some icterids are increasing in numbers and vitality. The Red-winged Blackbird, now among the most abundant of North American birds, has extended its range to Alaska, as has the Brown-headed Cowbird.

The Red-winged Blackbird has succeeded, primarily, because of its gregarious nature. Its genus name, "Agelaius," from the Greek and Latin, means "belonging to a flock." In summer, males and females congregate in nesting colonies of varying size. In winter, the sexes separate. Mixing with other blackbirds and European Starlings, they form populations numbering sometimes into the millions. What with winter plumage, different ages, and different species represented, members of such a mega flock can be difficult to identify: An individual does not stand out, but the totality impresses—and protects.

Aggressive, the Red-winged Blackbird will chase off predators such as raccoons, foxes, skunks, and raptors by "ganging up." It battles with marsh wrens, whose eggs it eats, and will attack potential predators as large as people and horses.

It has succeeded, further, because of its adaptability. Omnivorous in diet, the Red-winged Blackbird can find forage almost any place and, in difficulty, move on to new possibilities. In winter, it eats mostly seeds and grains and in summer, a wider diet of fruit, beetles, butterflies, moths, grasshoppers, ants, spiders, snakes, snails, frogs, eggs, carrion, worms, and mollusks. It will even eat fledgling birds.

Polygamous in breeding, the male will mate with up to 15 females in his territory, though those females will also mate with other males, producing clutches of mixed paternity. A male's territory may produce a population only half his: a system which seems to provide optimum opportunity for reproductive success and genetic strength.

Clever, the male uses his dramatic coloring—his shoulder epaulets—to warn other males away from his chosen area. Depending on circumstances, he can also choose not to show his colors. This way he creates and maintains his territory— the item which attracts females—usually about an eighth to a quarter of an acre.

Comfortable nesting in almost any small wet area—ditch or field—the redwing is also careful to build over water or in dense foliage for protection. Most predation of the bird occurs on nestlings. If one falls into the water, it can be eaten by bullfrogs, water snakes, or snapping turtles.

For its nest, the female weaves a cup-shaped basket of grasses and moss, lined with mud, bound to cattails or rushes and usually located over water for protection. She lays in it three to five pale blue eggs streaked with black, as if marked by pen and ink. Although she is the principal source of food for the young, the male will also assist in feeding. He is also more likely to help the first female to settle in his territory. The young fledge in 11 to 14 days and are independent in two to three weeks.

The female will raise two or three broods per season, each with a new nest, a sanitary exercise to cut down on parasites. Juveniles reach maturity in two years and mature birds in the wild live to an average of 2.14 years. The oldest known specimen lived to 15 years, 9 months.

Gregarious, adaptable, flexible, aggressive, and clever, the Red-winged Blackbird has surged with human population across the United States, taking advantage of the land we have opened up. In return, it helps us by controlling insect populations, especially since it eats such a wide variety. But, this symbiotic relationship is skewed: We serve not only as partner but also as enemy, vying for the same nesting areas and locked in endless skirmish over the same crops. From toxic waste to cell-phone towers, we endanger its well-being and represent its greatest threat. We fill ditches, roadsides, and waterways with beer cans and trash. We push the temperature higher and force a constant immigration into higher latitudes, always in the shadow of the Passenger Pigeon, the Carolina Parakeet, and the Ivory-billed Woodpecker.

These were my people, the Red-winged Blackbird People, stretching across the continent, testing new places and remaking themselves, beating their way across borders of time and space. Such was the flock with which my mother had flown and with which I was now flying, seeking information about what was ahead, the name and coordinates of the place we were destined to reach and settle.

I remember hearing how my Uncle Bradford McGuire survived by eating seaweed on a Pacific island after a battle in the Second World War. Later, he joined the Trappist order as a novice monk. He bequeathed his estate to near relatives, including me, and withdrew into that land of silence. Before taking his final vows, however, he resigned, returned to the Army, was stationed in Germany, and married. His wife never wanted their children to intermingle with his siblings and their offspring. Thus we lost track of our cousins. I never learned why. Our vagrant uncle—"Braddy" we called him—flew out of sight. I remember him as a tall, gentle spoken and kind man with a crew cut.

Red-winged Blackbird: A Vantage Point

A blackbird speaks with many voices—from the rusty creaking of the grackle to the welcome song of the meadowlark—and comes with many colors, in plain dress and fancy. Over the United States on any given day, the chances of observing a blackbird are high, the possibility of learning from a blackbird substantial.

The ones I watch in winter frequent a particular site on the South Carolina coast.

More specifically, it is a patch of lawn on the bank of a tidal creek separated by acres of smooth cordgrass (*Spartina alterniflora*) from the Beaufort River as it bends north towards the Coosaw River, the route of the Intracoastal Waterway. This home of ours is set on Lady's Island, an island within a world of islands, almost too many to count. Across the grass and water to the west, where the evening sun sets in fire, is the historic town of Beaufort, home of Secession, on Port Royal Island. To the east and south, linked by Route 21, or the Sea Island Parkway, lie the islands of St. Helena, Harbor, Hunting, and Fripp. To the south and west, across Port Royal Sound, lies Parris Island, famous home of the Marine Corps Recruit

Depot, or boot camp; further to the southwest, across Port
Royal Sound, lies Hilton Head Island, famous home of golf.
These are the major islands. Others—who can tell for sure
where solid land begins or ends?—crowd the map, often with
provocative names: Cane, Cat, Distant, Lost. Beaufort County
contains more than 2,000 of these shifting bits of topography,
a moving herd lashed by weather and hard to contain in any
map.

The Sea Islands stretch from Cumberland Island on the
Florida-Georgia line to Pawleys Island on the border between
North and South Carolina. Some large, some small, some mere
dots on the map, they appear on paper to be broken pieces of
a necklace. They are all in danger of breaking by storm, tide,
and erosion. Even more fragile are the barrier islands that protect them from the open ocean.

This is the land known as the *lowcountry*, the coastal estua-
rine edge where sea and river meet and at times are indistinguishable, where what appears solid earth moves and changes
shape and boundaries are indistinct. Tide, running six to seven
feet, as well as storms and shifting sand—all challenge the accuracy of any chart.

This is the opposite of *upcountry*, the inland area that
stretches towards the high ground of the Piedmont and eventually, the Appalachian Mountains.

This is the land of the salt marsh, an uncertain habitat
where blackbirds flourish—-a suitable place to search for my
mother and all those who had gone ahead into the pale lands
of no map and no name.

Where Birds and People Merge

When you watch for birds, you look for patterns. If you know what to expect, such as what birds might be found in certain settings and seasons, it is easier to identify and confirm what you see. History is similar. It is important to know what has happened in a place in order to know what you might expect to encounter and give name to what you experience. That which transpires ("breathes through") in a specific place never entirely disappears but lives on with an energy we have not yet been able to identify.

The history of my marsh home along the Beaufort River is long and extraordinarily complex——a tangle of Spanish and British adventurers; French Huguenots and other seekers of religious freedom; pirates and slaves; indigenous people and foreign entrepreneurs. Replete with ghosts, myths, and legends, this history could take me in many directions. I wondered if it would distract me from my course, or, like a rip tide, carry me away.

Today, after centuries of convoluted and bloody upheaval, Beaufort is changing again. Retirees, seeking the mild weather of the southeast coast, have moved in from Vermont, Michigan, Ohio, and the high plains, changing the demography and straining the infrastructure. Golf communities, with their gated entrances, have become the new plantations; Massa is now likely to be a corporation, perhaps Japanese or Saudi, and the overseer the bank wielding the mortgage. Agriculture has given way to military preparedness; and, where agriculture continues in the state, tobacco is giving way to crops of feverfew, valerian, and echinacea.

Tourists come with visions, often bolstered by book and movie: *Gone with the Wind* and, more recently, *Midnight in the Garden of Good and Evil.* Under the live oaks there is still evidence of the old south and much whispering in the leaves that constantly fall at the feet of these venerable trees. In the marshes, the grasses are constantly moving and much is indistinct. Where does land end and sea begin? It depends on where you stand and how you focus. At dusk, whippoorwill, tailor of darkness, sits at the edge of night crying its mournful call while sewing up the sunset sky.

In an area some say is more haunted than any other in the country, ghost tours have become a niche business. I took one in Beaufort on a bitterly cold winter's night.

Led on foot by a young woman in revealing Revolutionary dress with only a shawl covering her exposed shoulders and décolletage, we walked by the light of her battery-operated eighteenth-century lantern through the dark back streets of the oldest houses and the strangest stories. With Spanish moss (which, as the residents are quick to point out, is neither Spanish

nor moss but an air plant) billowing over our heads from the
huge live oaks and our guide's preternatural anecdotes grip-
ping us like the undeniable cold, we were ready to see or
believe anything. We ended our tour in the graveyard of St.
Helena's Episcopal Church, originally built between 1724 and
1726.

There, we approached a curious grave up against an outer
wall. At its foot fly two small British flags and the tombstone
offers two names—"Lieutenant William Calderwood and En-
sign John Finley of Colonel Prevost's British troops, killed in
battle near Gray's Hill, February 3, 1779, buried here February
5, 1779." The people of Beaufort had insisted on a decent and
dignified Christian burial, as well as one that would pay perma-
nent homage to the victims' native home.

The story continues. During the Civil War, when Beaufort
was designated as a hospital town and churches as operating
rooms and tombstones as operating tables, a pair of Union
soldiers on medical duty came out of the church for a smoke
break. Looking over the graveyard, they spotted a most unusual sight: two soldiers wearing the uniforms of the British
military of eighty years before. Calling others, they went to
investigate. The redcoats disappeared as the Union soldiers
approached, but not before they had been clearly seen by a
number of Union troops willing to testify to the event. And so
the British soldiers became one of the documented cases of
apparition to be told over and over in Beaufort: a fitting mix
of two wars, violent death, gentlemanliness, Christian charity,
and ghosts.

As a footnote, we were told how, when a member of the local and numerous Barnwell family is laid to rest in the ancestral
tombs, small orbs of light dance around the Barnwell graves.

This is the land where doors and shutters are painted blue
to keep out ghosts. This is the land between. This is where I
would start, on the edge of discovery.

I was already partly there because I had grown up in an
eighteenth-century house in Oyster Bay, New York—a town
occupied by the British during the American Revolution, a
place rife with soldiers, spies, ghosts, and history.

Once, during a family Christmas party, two guests watched a
pair of soldiers in Revolutionary attire walk through a wall into
our midst. Both guests were known for their psychic powers,
and with their help, the rest of us had no trouble imagining what
they described: two young men, cold and hungry, looking for
fellowship in a house that used to be a tavern, longing for the
warmth and companionship of home an ocean and war away.

There were other signs as well: With some frequency,
sounds and lights emanated from a small family cemetery on
our property. Usually, these manifestations were tied to a date
of death listed on one grave. According to the tombstone, it
contained a heart, the body buried at sea.

One Christmas Eve (again it was Christmas), a nebulous
ghost-shaped light persisted in the cemetery until we children
fled in fright from watching it. Yes, there were beings who
could walk through walls or make themselves known after
centuries.

Still, there was a reluctance to name these phenomena, much less speculate on what may have been their home. What I did absorb was the persistence of love and longing, their ability to transcend time and space.

Now, although a resident of Alaska, I had come to live part of each year in this richly woven place of coastal Carolina. At first, it seemed foreign. I had no connections with the south and felt an enormous political and philosophical divide. It was simply a place to be warm, or warmer than I would have been in my Alaskan home, and I felt alone, a variant pushed off course.

But the more I looked out over the marsh of the lowcountry, the more I saw that connected me with its history and gave me a sense of where I stood in the universe. My father's family had been French Huguenot, aligning me with Jean Ribaut, one of the earliest claimants; and my mother's family were Irish Catholics, the energetic interlopers. In me, these warring factions merged, never quite put to rest, and now, with a divided heart, I would go in search of all that had been lost.

Robert Penn Warren's lament seemed a good beginning:

> *Grackles, goodbye! The sky will be vacant and lonely*
> *Till again I hear your horde's rusty creak high above,*
> *Confirming the year's turn and the fact that only, only*
> *In the name of Death do we learn the true name of Love.*
> *("Grackles, Goodbye")*

But naming love was not enough. The poet also acknowledged, "I longed to know the world's name."

To know the world's name and the name of the world to come——that was what I was after. That was my mission, but how could I start? How could I find the courage to set forth on such an expedition, alone? Who could possibly lead me?

John White
(1540?-1606?)

Blessed with time during a cold winter visit to the Carolina coast, I read what I could find on the history of this mysterious place. I wanted the early history——the time when little was known and almost everything was to be learned. When I came across John White referred to as the "governor of the lost," I latched onto him immediately. Who could possibly be better than a leader who was lost: John White (1540?-1606?), Governor of the Roanoke Colony.

Never was there a traveler more cursed than John White, governor of the lost. Even accurate dates for his life cannot be established.

A British limner, or watercolorist, he made the first of five voyages to "Virginia," now known as North Carolina, in 1584. The following year he served as artist to Sir Walter Ralegh's first effort to establish a colony at Roanoke on the Outer Banks under the governance of Ralph Lane. During that trip, he was accompanied by mathematician Thomas Harriot, a scientific observer. Together, they studied, mapped, sketched, and described their location.

Meanwhile, the 108 settlers at Roanoke found themselves in increasingly desperate circumstances. They were unprepared for life in the wilderness and grew antagonistic toward the native inhabitants. Then, almost a year later in June 1586, Sir Francis Drake serendipitously appeared off the coast of Roanoke Island offering aid. Drake had recently attacked and overwhelmed the Spanish stronghold of St. Augustine. On his way north he had, for some reason, missed the fort on Parris Island and sailed on to the Roanoke colony.

A storm came up, and Drake's men wanted to leave as quickly as possible, forcing the colonists into a hurried departure. In the confusion, trunks of papers were lost to the surf, including some of White's watercolors and many of Harriot's specimens and seeds. Three colonists, off on a hunting party, were abandoned.

Several days after Drake pulled the colonists away so precipitously, Ralegh's supply ship arrived at Roanoke. After assessing the situation, the captain quickly departed. Within weeks, the next scheduled group of colonists landed, discovered the situation, and decided also to leave, except for fifteen men who stayed behind to hold the site. Along with the three from the original colony, there now were eighteen Englishmen alone in the wilderness.

When White returned to Roanoke in 1587, Ralegh had appointed him Governor. New among the colonists White had been able to prevail upon to join the venture were his pregnant daughter, Eleanor, and son-in-law, Ananias Dare. The party was not intending to settle at Roanoke, where there had already been so much trouble. The goal was to settle further north, in Chesapeake Bay.

The party planned simply to stop at Roanoke to pick up the fifteen colonists left as custodians the year before and possibly the three who had been abandoned earlier. But when they arrived, Roanoke revealed nothing but one skeleton. White's troublesome sailing master Simon Fernandez, more interested in privateering in the Caribbean than colonizing, refused to go on. White, unequal to the challenge, gave up the plans for Chesapeake Bay and settled his party down to repair the moldering huts of their predecessors.

On August 18, soon after the colonists disembarked, Eleanor gave birth to her daughter, Virginia Dare, the first English child born in the New World. (Later, colonist Margery Harvey also gave birth.) Nine days after his granddaughter's birth, White hurriedly left for England.

He had been persuaded to return for essential supplies but also knew he had been forced out with a vote of no confidence. Pushed into another quick departure—Fernandez had stayed anchored offshore for unknown reasons—White left behind a party of 112, including his newborn granddaughter. These he carefully listed, the names divided into "Men," "Women," "Boys and Children," and "Children Born in Virginia"—a life list for all times.

The date was August 27: already the threshold of winter on the perilous edge of the wilderness. White's ill-fated return to England approached disaster. Beset by months of misadventures, he finally arrived home, by way of Ireland, in November.

There, he found that war with Spain had taken center stage and fear of the Armada had overwhelmed any other seafaring interests. Queen Elizabeth impressed every vessel. He finally wangled two tiny ships considered worthless for engaging the Spaniards and set sail to return to Roanoke in April 1588, pirating along the way. French pirates with larger ships attacked his small fleet, forcing White to return to England, where he became landlocked once again. Only after Ralegh and Drake routed the Armada in the summer of 1588 could White begin to hope again that he might return to Roanoke and his family.

But prospects for colonizers were dim. It took until March 1590 before Ralegh could gain permission to send two ships back to America and White could hitch a ride—his fifth voyage to Virginia. Once more, it was as much a privateering expedition as a colonizing effort, an arduous journey that took five months. They arrived on his granddaughter's third birthday.

On their way into Roanoke Island, one of the two ship's boats capsized and the captain and six other men drowned. Approaching the settlement, White found the letters "CRO" carved in a tree. To greet him at the site of the abandoned and overgrown settlement, he found only the word "Croatoan" etched on a post.

Because there was no Maltese cross—a code he and the colonists had decided upon as a mark of departure under duress—he assumed they had gone to the home of the Croatoans, a small tribe who lived on what is now known as Hatteras Island. He urged the expedition leader to follow but met only obstacles and resistance. With the approach of stormy weather, fear of the dangerous coastline, and the loss of anchors, the decision was made to sail to the Caribbean for the winter and return to Croatoan in the spring.

Fate intervened again. Their misnamed ship, the *Hopewell*, was blown to the Azores and the expedition was abandoned. White's search was over. His quest would have to be taken up by others as interest and will allowed. But the lost colony has never been found.

Ironically, it was also in 1590 that White's watercolors became famous when Frankfurt engraver Theodor de Bry copied and reproduced them as copper-plate engravings to illustrate a new edition of Harriot's *A Briefe and True Report of the New Found Land of Virginia*, first published on its own in 1588.

The elaborate production—Volume I of a series titled *Grand Voyages*, or *America*, awakened great interest in the natural history of the New World. Unfortunately, de Bry had taken many liberties with the illustrations. White's unadulterated watercolors would not be published until the twentieth century.

White states on the title page of his collection: "THE pictures of sondry things collected and counterfeited according to the truth in the voyage made by Sr: Walter Raleigh knight...." Linguists point out that "counterfeit" did not then carry the same negative connotations it carries today but indicated instead a recreation on paper.

Among White's 35 drawings of birds are the Common Grackle, the Northern Oriole, and the Red-winged Blackbird.

Already blackbird was becoming one of the most studied and well-known birds of America.

The history of White's artistry and his record of birds is easier to track than his personal story, which fades at this point to conjecture. What seethed in the artist's shipwrecked heart can only be imagined: a map of pain known only to himself.

What followed, chronologically, was a curious history of dreams, hopes, and brutality, best portrayed by Giles Milton in his book, *Big Chief Elizabeth: The Adventures and Fate of the First English Colonists in America.*

As Milton explains: White, broken, repaired to an estate of Ralegh's in Ireland, where he was last heard from in 1593, in a letter to Richard Hakluyt pertaining to his final voyage: "Thus committing the reliefe of my discomfortable company the planters in Virginia, to the merciful help of the Almighty, whom I most humbly beseech to help and comfort them."

Ralegh, losing favor with the Queen, was imprisoned and ignored for five years. Only in 1599 was he able to take up the search for his lost Roanoke colonists. Over the next several years, he launched three expeditions which failed to reach their target, while a fourth, led by Samuel Mace, came back in unfortunate times. It was the summer of 1603, a time of plague and dispersal. Elizabeth had died and the dour James I, no friend of colonization, had returned Ralegh to the Tower. Mace seemed to bring back news that the Roanoke colonists lived, but there was no one to take up their cause. Rumors persisted. Years passed.

In April 1606, a Virginia Company expedition of three ships entered Chesapeake Bay to establish the Jamestown settlement. One of the party was John Smith, famously saved by Pocahontas from the death sentence leveled by her father, the powerful chief Powhatan. Years later, Smith would publicly reveal what Powhatan told him before Smith's aborted execution: Powhatan had had a band of Roanoke survivors butchered as Smith's ship arrived in the bay. Some escaped.

Some also came to life as mythic figures, foremost among them Virginia Dare. The subject of coastal Carolina folklore, Virginia Dare became known as the "Ghost Deer of Roanoke," a symbol of transformation: When the white doe said to roam Roanoke is shot with a charmed arrow to her heart, she turns back into Virginia Dare for a moment and then dies. Numerous versions of this tale are still told. Names and narratives change, but never the theme: Virginia Dare lives. Her people continue.

Alongside Virginia Dare, Pocahontas quickly rose from history to legend to the elevated status of myth. Without her interference and her rescue of John Smith, we would never have learned of Chief Powhatan's declaration that the Roanoke colonists, or some of them at least, lived on.

There were other survivors as well, in the place White had foretold——Croatoan——but was never able to reach. And there was more corroborating news as well, news that would come from my second guide.

John White, though lost, had provided essential information. Clearly I needed another guide as well, one more accessible——someone closer in time and with more of a written record. Above all, it had to be someone living on the edge of discovery—someone not afraid to venture into the unknown and name the nameless. Without hesitation I chose John Lawson (?-1711).

John Lawson
(?-1711)

Lawson, like White, appeared out of nowhere; there is no conclusive information to establish the place or date of his birth. He came to the New World almost by coincidence when a stranger convinced him to take passage on a ship bound for Carolina. We do know that he landed in Charles Town (now Charleston, South Carolina) in August, 1700, and soon set off on the adventure that would culminate in *A New Voyage to Carolina*, a book that would be read with interest hundreds of years later.

In his decade devoted to exploration and development of the Carolinas, he gave us significant information on not only the flora and fauna of the coast but also the indigenous people, who were quickly being exterminated by the incursion of Europeans. His particular connection was with the Tuscaroras of eastern Carolina.

Lawson was perceptive and precise, an explorer not afraid of tangled waterways and changing coastlines: I could trust him.

In one of those inexplicable crossovers that haunt early expeditions of discovery, Lawson traveled to Hatteras Island (Croatoan) in 1701 and interviewed local Indians who told him that some of their ancestors were white people who could read, or "talk in a Book." These people, he was told, had gray eyes, valued their likeness to the English, and were ready to offer Englishmen "all friendship." Of these Lawson surmised:

> *It is probable, that this Settlement miscarry'd for want of timely Supplies from England; or thro' the Treachery of the Natives, for we may reasonably suppose that the English were forced to cohabit with them, for Relief and Conversation; and that in the process of Time, they conform'd themselves to the Manners of their Indian Relations. And thus we see, how apt Humane Nature is to degenerate.*
> (Lawson, p. 69)

Immediately after this unkind portrayal of the Hatteras Indians, Lawson added the following curious paragraph:

> *I cannot forbear inserting here, a pleasant Story that passes for an uncontested Truth amongst the Inhabitants of this Place; which is, that the Ship which brought the first Colonies, does often appear amongst them, under Sail, in a gallant Posture, which they call Sir Walter Raleigh's Ship; And the truth of this has been affirm'd to me, by Men of*

the best Credit in the Country.
(Lawson, p. 69)

What was this apparition?

In February 1973, shortly after I moved to Alaska, crewmen aboard the Alaska state ferry *Malaspina* officially recorded in the log the following account of sighting a gossamer ship:

> The ship's position when sighting was abeam of Twin Island, Revillagigedo Channel. The time was 0655 hours Pacific Standard time. The weather was clear with unlimited visibility. Wind Northeast 10 knots, temperature 28 degrees, and the barometer pressure was 30.71.
>
> Standing watch on the bridge was Chief Mate Walter Jackinsky and two sailors—one at the helm and one lookout. A huge vessel was seen approximately eight miles dead ahead, broadside and dead in the water. This vessel resembled very much the *Flying Dutchman*. The color was all gray—similar to vapor or clouds. It was seen distinctly for about ten minutes. It looked so exact, natural and real that when seen through binoculars sailors could be seen moving on board. Within seconds it disappeared into oblivion.
>
> This is the first such sighting to any of these present, all of whom were in full agreement.
>
> (*Alaskan Southeaster Magazine,* July 1991)

As the years went by, I was to hear many tales of the *Fata Morgana*—an image created by the bending of light during a temperature inversion. I wondered if this explained Lawson's report of the sighting of Ralegh's ship. *Fata Morgana* have power. Shape-shifting, they have lured gullible explorers into expeditions to nowhere. Perhaps I was on one of those.

Field Notes and Questions

For birders, the field notebook is a tool for learning as well as recordkeeping. The purpose of taking notes in the field is to sharpen skills of observation and identification in order to be able to make and verify sight records quickly under less than optimum conditions. To take good field notes requires patience, accuracy, veracity, and evidence. First, you must truly see the bird and write down its characteristics: You must counterfeit "according to the truth."

Then, as you make the determination, there are many other points to take into account: field guides and references consulted; lighting conditions and weather; habitat; distance from subject; previous experience; field marks, songs, calls, activity, and behavior observed; chronology; type of lens used; location; geography; landmarks; corroborators; seasonal color changes; consideration of confusing similar species. Of overarching importance, ethical conditions must be maintained. A bird that is only heard and not seen counts for some lists but not for others.

Besides personal lists, there are always official surveys and counts underway in search of help, such as the Audubon

Christmas Bird Count, held from December 14 to January 5 each year. Accurate notes from the field can move beyond the page to help define the health and range of a species. Sometimes notes can mark a journey into the unknown, building a record of the unnamed.

I needed to concentrate and write careful notes. How else could I remember, when my memory could all too easily fail me? No matter what the distractions, I needed to pay attention. If Lawson could focus in spite of storms and roaring rivers, surely I could emulate him amid much more comfortable circumstances.

It is difficult, however, when the universe is constantly moving out from its center and black holes implode around us. The enormity of space grows beyond imagining, while large new galaxies continue to be born, and physics continues to be rewritten. We learn that the sub-atomic, or unseen, is remarkably different from what we perceive everyday with our senses—what we call the physical world. We learn how many billions of microbes exist and how many more undoubtedly exist which we will never know, and we are easily awed into a sense of hopelessness: How could we, against this immense background, matter? My twelve-year-old grandson stated confidently, "The universe is so large that nothing on earth matters," meaning that no event on earth, no matter how cataclysmic, can have an effect on any other part of the universe. We are that small.

Perhaps nothing we do can have an effect, but we must go on, pushing against dark matter, to reach the realm where blackbird nests, at the edge of mystery—that liminal realm where solid is not solid and the shore is never certain. From here, blackbird surges north to find new breeding territory and carry forth its line, before ultimately turning into something else, flying off the map, and losing all labels. What is the name of the world? When is a planet not a planet, and how do we describe what we cannot see—or what is not there?

According to Arctic historian W. Gillies Ross, a clerk in the British Colonial Office in 1853 referred to the southeastern part of Baffin Island as "this distant and unsurveyed country."

We might find no better description for the land we travel towards, wherever it might be

Mark Catesby
(c.1683-1749)

To gain some perspective, I turned to yet another guide: Mark Catesby (c.1683-1749), an itinerant naturalist-explorer-artist who might be considered a pioneer in the field of ecology. Catesby, I hoped, could show me the bigger picture—how things fit together. He was known for the accurate pairing in his drawings of bird or mammal with flora.

When Catesby, a gentleman from Sudbury, England, arrived in Williamsburg, Virginia, on April 23, 1712, he had immediate access to the scientific community of a flourishing colonial town. He had come as the guest of his sister Elizabeth and brother-in-law William Cocke, a physician. Welcomed into their world of well-to-do and scientifically inclined colonists, he quickly put to work the horticultural knowledge he had gained through acquaintance and communication with some of the leading natural historians of his day such as John Ray and George Edwards.

As he translated his English botanical experience into an understanding of the gardens and plantations of Virginia, he began to study birds and animals and their association with plants. Extending his range, he traveled in 1714 to Jamaica and other islands of the West Indies.

Although Catesby's first visit to the colonies lasted seven years, he chastised himself for not working more systematically and thus productively. It was only after he returned to London, he claimed, and made the friendship of botanist William Sherard, that he began to envision the structure of his studies: publication of *The Natural History*. In this major work, Catesby would manifest his vision of relationships in the natural world. And it was here that he established the foundation of American ornithology.

But first, he would have to return from London to the colonies. In order to do so, he needed to obtain backers and underwriters for his proposed expedition—a lengthy process.

When Catesby finally arrived in Charles Town on May 23, 1722, he found, in comparison with Williamsburg, a much less well-established town, one close enough to the frontier still to be fending off foreign invaders, indigenous tribes, and pirates. (It was only four years after the infamous Edward Teach or Blackbeard had blockaded the harbor and cowed the city.) As with his visit to Williamsburg, however, the newly arrived artist soon became familiar with the gardens and plantations of the prominent residents; and these residents wanted to know what lay beyond their cultivated grounds.

To satisfy their interests and those of his backers in England, Catesby started traveling—first, three times up the Savannah River to Fort Moore, near what would become Augusta, Georgia. Then in 1725, he ventured to the Bahamas. It was there that he observed and explained that Bobolinks (or "rice-birds," as he and Lawson called them) migrated in winter in order to follow the rice crops from Carolina to Cuba. At the time, it was still widely accepted that birds disappeared in winter because they were hibernating under water or in caves. Some even maintained they flew to the moon. Though he could not explain the complexities of migration because, Catesby said, of "the immenseness of the globe" and "the vast tracts of land remaining unknown but to its barbarous natives," he was ready to end the conjecture of what happened to birds that disappeared in the cold months:

> *The reports of their lying torpid in caverns and hollow trees, and of their resting in the same state at the bottom of deep waters, are notions so ill attested and absurd in themselves, that they deserve no farther notice.*
> (Catesby, p.163)

In 1726, Catesby returned to London to finance and produce his *magnum opus*. While working as a horticulturist to support his family, he continued to acquire new specimens from the colonies to incorporate into his studies. His former backers, pleased with his efforts, renewed their support, while new ones joined the campaign. Altogether, more than 150 subscribers on both sides of the Atlantic committed to his project of visually documenting the nature of the New World.

Still, there was not enough money to take the drawings to the master engravers of Amsterdam or Paris. Catesby was forced to take the arduous route of learning the process of engraving himself. Working with London printmaker Joseph Goupy, he began to produce his two volumes. The first, published between 1729 and 1732, he devoted to birds and dedicated to Queen Caroline, known for her interest in gardening. The second volume was published between 1734 and 1743.

The Natural History of Carolina, Florida and the Bahama Islands included 220 color plates of birds, reptiles, amphibians, fishes, insects, mammals, and plants, and was hailed as a monumental achievement which would enter into numerous editions. Linnaeus, Thomas Jefferson, Lewis and Clark, and John James Audubon would consult it and make use of it.

When Catesby died two years after publication, his resources were exhausted. His widow was forced to sell remaining copies and plates in order to survive.

Catesby is remembered today as the first person to draw and describe the Wood Duck (which he called the Summer Duck, *Aix sponsa*). The bullfrog (*Rana catesbeiana*), which he introduced to the Old World, now carries his name in the New. A duck and a frog: For all his effort Catesby did not get much return and only recently has his work gained serious attention.

Maria Sybilla Merian
(1647-1727)

I wasn't looking for her. I barely knew her name, but she kept popping up in my search for guidance among the early naturalists. She was clearly an inspiration to those, like Catesby, who followed her, and she quickly became an inspiration for me: Maria Sybilla Merian (1647-1727), the Dutch artist who identified the miracle of metamorphosis.

At a time when it was believed that insects arose spontaneously from mud, she depicted and explained how they developed and how—as no one before her had observed—they interacted with their environment. At a time when women did not travel without a male escort, she set out for Surinam, the former Dutch colony on the northeast Atlantic coast of South America, in June 1699, a year before Lawson sailed for Charles Town and 16-year-old Catesby had yet to set sail for America.

Long since divorced, she was accompanied by a daughter and under the titular protection of the captain. For two years she studied and painted the jungle creatures in their natural settings. Only malaria persuaded her to return home.

When poverty prevented publication of her books, she learned engraving, as Catesby did. Although she could manage to produce only a few of her own plates, she also produced work-for-hire, illustrating the work of others as a means to raise funds for her own. As with Catesby, the final chapter of her life was spent trying to publish what she had so ardently set as her goal: a major study of how flora and fauna interact. And, as with Catesby, she died in poverty.

Metamorphosis Insectorum Surinamensium appeared in 1705, with 60 plates. A second book on reptiles and other animals of Surinam failed to take form, but a second edition of *Metamorphosis* was published in 1719, two years after her death.

In 1715, as Catesby continued to explore the southeastern colonies, Merian suffered a debilitating stroke. On the last day of her life—January 13, 1717—an agent of Peter the Great finished negotiations with her family in Amsterdam for the purchase of nearly 300 of her watercolors. And so, as Merian crossed over into the unknown, her brilliant tropical insects and winged creatures began to migrate east across the frozen landscape of Europe to the icy heart of Russia. The Czar would continue to acquire more of her paintings until he had the largest Merian collection in the world, followed by that of the royal family of England. Her life-long journal would rest there, too, a chrysalis in the archives of St. Petersburg, until it was rediscovered in 1976 and allowed to take wing into a larger world.

I needed to know she was there—at least hovering over my own journey. If Maria Sybilla Merian could turn her life into such a voyage of discovery, surely I could learn something of our purpose in traveling this world, exploring its mysterious entrances and exits.

An Empty Day

My guides would have much to do. They might quit me at any moment, especially since I could offer them nothing. In the meantime, I would set out, taking my chances.

I remember one particularly cold, windy winter's day on the Carolina coast. The lawn was empty. The creek was also empty, a flight of Brown Pelicans having just departed. (Remembering Psalm 102, Lawson called this bird the "Pellican of the Wilderness"—*I am like a pelican of the wilderness; I am like an owl of the desert"*— and commented of the Tuscarora that "They make Tobacco-pouches of his Maw.") The sky was empty, too, quieting after a brace of F/A-18's from the nearby Marine Air Station had roared by. The canvas appeared empty, as if the naturalist-explorer-artist in charge had painted the background and walked about waiting, considering what subject to impose. But this was a place of watercolors, not oils or acrylics: Everything happened at once, not stage by stage, and was in constant flux.

My intuition hinted that the subject I was missing was already here; I simply had not yet become conscious of it. If I had the enthusiasm of the early itinerant naturalists, I would find it: a particular grass, or shell; or perhaps something as dramatic as a Wood Stork. To find that elusive subject, should I track the itinerant naturalists or the Indians, the pirates or the planters, the slaves or the soldiers?

The subject was present. I grew sure of this. If I were honest and applied my fullest concentration, I would see it. I would turn towards the canvas with its browns and blues and *see*. I would start recording. I would develop a new taxonomy, a new language, breaking beyond Linnaeus, and find a way to pin it down: the true name of All There Is: the true name of Love.

I would make mistakes. I would forge ahead. I would find my own path out into the marsh. I would fall down. I would get up. Be laughed at. I would invite others to come along, try different guides, change canoes. I would be lost sometimes in the sorrowful fog that hangs over the winter marsh. I would look for clues, knowing that the secret might be in sounds, not sights. I would try to remember the tide in order not to be caught by it. I would keep a clock in my heart but not in front of me. (I would remember that Linnaeus attempted a clock of flowers.) I would find the edge of the circle of blackbird, the place where the inner and outer merge, the place where solid dissolves and where you see with other than eyes.

The subject, I think, is memory; and my list, my personal Life List, is that of the faces and vignettes I remember. As I get older, I see more and more movement of such images just over the horizon. I need to know their names and where they live. Is it Croatoan where they have all fled, colony after colony, flock after flock, leaving few clues behind and all of us searching forever?

Ghosts

Of course, it was not so much that the marsh was filling with ghosts as my life was, but the marsh was where I now perched, looking out winter's day after winter's day, trying to determine what it was I was seeing. Who and what were these faces and figures playing across the grassy screen, my field of meditation?

It was not just the deaths piling up around me but the estrangements as well, a melancholy population off to one side, one with similar but slightly different markings from their kind. Ornithologist David Allen Sibley might call it "aberrant plumage." There was my father, who had been forced by circumstances to give up poetry for a career on Wall Street, which he came to hate. His vocalizations are harsh and haunting.

Standing with his back to me is my brother, a year older than I, who lived a sorrowful, hidden life with male partners he felt he could not publicly acknowledge: He kicks angrily in the sand as if for something that is not there. Then there is my older son who, for unfathomable reasons, decided to sever himself from the family. He watches the shallow water closely, waiting.

On occasion, these two species of the dead and the estranged merged in the marsh, as if in conversation. They would walk about, or float, leave, and return. I needed to compare them. What were their field marks? Their topography? Their behavior? What were they feeding on here? And where did they go when I no longer could see them? What did more experienced observers have to say? What quadrant of the map was this, what circle of blackbird? Could I lead other observers to them for verification? I might need further direction—psychics and mediums and those who could translate the soul and map the heart.

I have a neighbor who talks with spirits as he gardens. They are, he says, in a transitional place, waiting to move on. He gives them space. If they are gathered in a spot where he plans to do a project, he switches to another area, another task. He describes them to me specifically, but still they are invisible. The experienced birder, Sibley says, has learned to see details; the beginner, not.

I had a friend, a young man named Tim, whose apparition walked through our bedroom one night as he was dying by suicide several miles away across town. I saw him clearly and remember the sounds he made as he opened the closet door and turned on the light.

He walked across the bedroom, stopped and looked directly at Martin and me lying in bed, then proceeded to the door and faded through it. I knew it was Tim, but what had he become? I ran after him, but he was gone. I searched all over the house, hopelessly, and did not hear of his death until some hours later.

Birdwatchers know that they learn by mistake and that mistakes usually come from misidentifying common birds, not by failing to recognize rare birds.

I keep trying. What ornithologist David Allen Sibley says is this: "The first rule is simple. *Look at the bird.* Don't fumble with a book, because by the time you find the right picture the bird will most likely be gone." (*Field Guide to Birds of Eastern North America*, p. 10)

Books are essential, especially field guides, but I had fumbled with too many. I needed to start over. I needed advice from new guides. I could almost hear them whispering.

Blackbird: Its Absence

This morning there are no blackbirds on my Carolina lawn. There have not been any for some days. It has been windy and chilly. Perhaps they have found a more protected place, one back from the open expanses of marsh and water. Perhaps they have found and are feasting in an abundant field. I do not know. But the lawn is empty and my eyes cannot rest.

There is an occasional Great Egret (or perhaps a Snowy) that rises and sinks into the distant brown grasses between our creek and the river. I will not get binoculars. I am not looking for egrets. The sky this morning is brushed with clouds. Suddenly F/A-18's roar into action with a thrust that vibrates through the body. The world, once again, is close to war. My thoughts are shattered into pieces: Iraq, politics, economics, global destruction. Then I remember my guides—what they and the Native Americans they encountered had to suffer in a world of constant danger.

Lawson, among the Congerees, remarked how many people they had lost "by intestine Broils; but most by the Small-pox, which hath often visited them, sweeping away whole Towns." Early records indicate a pattern of epidemics along the coast: smallpox in 1677-78; yellow fever and small pox in 1699; yellow fever in 1706; small pox in 1711-12—a sad rubric to the history of the Carolinas.

To escape the fevers of summer, wealthy planters fled their upland homes for houses in the mountains or here, on the coast, leaving their overseers in charge of the vacated plantations. But the welcome breezes of the Sea Islands were no certain antidote. Fevers killed relentlessly, filling family burial plots with poignant groupings, long before the ravages of the Civil War.

Sometimes when we played golf, we came across these mournful hamlets fenced off from our play, and I think of the shadow children flitting over the marshlands with goldfinches in the twilight hours, playing hide and seek with those calling them helplessly home in the wing-filled dusk. One such place is part of the Dunes West Golf Club on Wagner Creek near Charleston, where an iron fence protects the antebellum graves of ten children and two adults.

If I could only ask these children: Where have you gone, bolting so quickly from your cribs and your nurseries, not even waiting for the war? The birdless sky, Robert Penn Warren says, will be "lonely and vacant."

But is it? Is the sky ever vacant? I think, instead, the air around us is a crowded world with wilderness and city, paths and rivers, explorations and expeditions, lists and field notes, sketches, and watercolors, oceans and discovery ships. It is also *Fata Morgana*.

Nineteenth-century Spiritualists called heaven "Summer Land," but how could they be certain that it did not contain winter, too? I'd rather think it is the Field of Everything, the crossroads of our multiverse, the place physicists are trying to define with that one elegant—or simple—formula that evades them—the name of the world plus the name of Love which keeps the world from flying apart. If physics (from the Greek word for "natural things") is the study of matter and its interactions with energy, then what do we call the search beyond the realms of matter? What would Linnaeus say?

Fighter jets suddenly careen by again, off their regular flight path (a matter carefully mapped and posted in the rear offices of Beaufort real estate companies), and crows dart out of the marsh. I jump up, startled as the crows. It seems the nature of thought is to be disturbed by threats and distractions. In the wake of the roar, a pelican flaps by, angling to find balance in the wind.

I recall a line from Psalm 102, a prayer of the afflicted: "I watch, and am as a sparrow alone upon the house top."

What We Are Searching for

When you look for birds, you are not alone. Even when you see no motion and hear no sound, you know they are nearby. Sometimes you can "Pish" and call them up. Sometimes you must simply be patient. However hidden, they are there. Like the object in the block of stone which the sculptor releases, they are there.

I think what we want most of all is not to be alone.

Usually, when we go in search of birds, we go in groups. There are many reasons—safety, the need for educational leadership, shared resources and information, possibilities for instant verification, corroboration, and, simply, companionship. We do not want to be by ourselves when we discover something of wonder. If we are alone, we immediately think of all those with whom we would like to share the experience. We hurry out of the woods-jungle-desert to proclaim our find. We seek our flock and tell our story. Storytelling is what connects us and keeps us part of the tribe. Storytelling is what reinforces memory and defines our species. It validates our legacy and clarifies our itinerary. It serves as a signpost on the way. Searching, discovering, sharing: This is our work.

Even when there are no blackbirds and the lawn looks vacant and lonely, the air is not. The air is the great invisible continent, the country of everything, and everywhere we stand is its shore. Chief Seattle, of my northwestern home, is said to have stated that every place is filled with memories and spirits: "In all the earth there is no place dedicated to solitude."

Birdwatchers come to the edge. But they know too that eventually they must follow their subject inside—whatever lies beyond the boundary. Sailors have a different way of putting it: Eventually, they say, you have to leave the harbor.

I wanted to follow blackbird, my species, into new areas where we could find a living and thrive. For too long we had been splitting up and weakening, losing property, losing influence, losing stature and recognition. I did not know my cousins and could barely say their names. I wanted my flock to flourish, and I wanted to flourish with them. It was time to push forward, crossing borders, but to where?

Memory

Increasingly, scientists tell us how unreliable memory is—how malleable—that it is always reworking itself through the context of the present. Witnesses to an event experience quite different scenes; their reports cannot be trusted and in legal settings carry little weight. Our minds, unlike computers, do not lock in place what we see and hear. Rather, they recreate it, constantly. Memory is kinetic, not static. But what happens to those pieces of memory that are changed beyond recognition or lost? Where does an orphan memory go? Is there some place like Croatoan where it hides or a hospital where it is treated?

What causes my brain to see these specters that cavort over the marsh, or do they, indeed, invade my mind and force themselves there where egrets rise? Do they hijack my brain? Surely no one else looking out over this particular marsh would see these same faces dwelling together in the cordgrass, yet these faces exist out there as surely as the birds that fly among them.

What is the difference between "memory" and "haunting"? When does a memory become a haunting, an image driven by longing that will not rest? And what of dreams, which we can learn to reconstruct, and imagination? Then, there is "obsession," the relentless power that drives. Can an obsession be so strong it splinters off at death and dwells between two worlds, running forever on its own energy, an orphaned electric imprint?

Perhaps Sir Walter Ralegh's ghost ship as reported by John Lawson was such an obsession. Perhaps John White's longing was that powerful. Does it, or could it, continue to appear today?

When Robert Peary of North Pole fame reported and named an unknown arctic country "Crocker Land," the American Museum of Natural History gave way to his insistence and launched a long and expensive expedition to find it (the Crocker Land Expedition, 1913-1917). Expedition leader Donald Baxter MacMillan declared at its outset: "Its boundaries and extent can only be guessed at, but I am certain that strange animals will be found there, and I hope to discover a new race of men."

Though he chased his phantasm over miles of frozen landscape, Macmillan's expedition never found a new race of men any more than a new landmass. At one point, Macmillan was convinced his goal was finally in sight: "There could be no doubt about it. Great heavens! What a land! Hills, valleys, snow-capped peaks extending through at least one hundred and twenty degrees of the horizon." But Pee-a-wah-to and E-took-a-shoo, his Inuit guides, assured him that what he saw was "poo-jok," or mist. (Macmillan, p. 80)

It took the Crocker Expedition four years to get home, cost hundreds of thousands of dollars, endured a murder,

intrigue, and incalculable suffering to men and to those al-
ways-forgotten partners, the sledge dogs. A *Fata Morgana* can
be that powerful.

Surely when White looked back across the Atlantic Ocean
from Ireland to Roanoke, he did not wish to see again the
Brown Pelicans, Common Grackles, Northern Orioles, and
Red-winged Blackbirds that once he worked so hard to record;
he longed for his infant granddaughter, his daughter, and his
son-in-law, as well as the other colonists from whom he had
become separated forever. Surely he continued to stare at that
word, "Croatoan," etched into the post and his mind forever.
It is not hard to imagine that it is he flashing that word back to
me now while trying to guide my search. It is not hard to imagine that he continues to send his ship even centuries later, not
letting me forget; for that is what we want—not to be forgotten and lost in the immensity of time and space. Meanwhile,
archaeologists are still digging, trying to find his village.

Memory: At the Gate of Heaven

On my mother's side, I come from a family of women who lose their memories early. When I was small, I thought all older women were vacant and childlike, needing a level of care that devoured those who gave it. People had to chase after them as they escaped from apartment buildings. People had to dress them and interpret for them, repeating conversations over and over. People had to be extremely patient, and always polite. As I grew older, I watched beautiful, intelligent women reduced to gibberish and round-the-clock surveillance. I was not horrified; I thought the process was normal. No one told me otherwise.

When we buried my mother, whose memory had long since fled, it was in a deep grave on top of her aunt, a woman of immense charm and wit who had lived without memory for many years. Now I was the generation on top, the sparrow alone on the roof. I still had my mind and a fair percentage of what it had filed away, but for how long?

As the oldest woman—and person—in my family, I had become the keeper of my mother's family burial plot at Gate of Heaven, the cemetery for the Catholic Archdiocese of New

York located outside the city in Hawthorne. The deed, taken out by my great-grandmother Emma F. Cuddihy in 1945, had been lost, but I gained access by an affidavit and was given a list of the interred, with the identifying numbers of section, lot, grave. Some of the names of the dead had not been etched on the tombstone, I discovered. Who could tell whose remains rested here in this silent household once so full of conversation? Now I had to make room for my mother and declare her presence in this edifice. I had only cemetery records to inform me, and how could I know if they were accurate? I hired a stonecutter and gave him directions.

What will happen if my memories, like my mother's, are eaten away and I lose the bridge between this world and the next? Suppose I command, like Vladimir Nabokov, Speak, Memory! and nothing happens?

Perhaps I could make something happen. I could follow the system of ornithology, moving from Gaviidae to Fringillidae, from loon to sparrow. As I wrote down my observations, made my identifications, and checked off the species, the singing world would grow increasingly vibrant around me. I would travel to find more, even chasing down the vagrants. As I struggled with taxonomy, I would exercise my mind. Learning foreign languages, it is said, protects the mind against the ravages of Alzheimer's; and I would be doing more. In studying and classifying memory, I would not only be learning a language but creating one. I also might study the language and brain of birds, a field ripe with newly discovered complexity, one now translated by sonogram instead of clef notes.

When I worked for the Alaska Department of Fish and Game, I had an acquaintance named Pete Isleib who helped me when I needed bird identification questions answered. An authority on the birds of Prince William Sound, he also had remarkable knowledge of the vagrants and Asian accidentals (birds outside their range recorded in only a few instances) which would be found on occasion in Alaska. During his life (1938-93), he held the record for the largest number of species observed in the state—387. He wrote articles for our conservation magazine and provided editorial advice. He always had a smile and always had time—he could untangle almost any twisted bird story or interpret any debatable photograph and would work unstintingly to share his knowledge. He traveled much of the time, both to fish commercially and to pursue his interest in ornithology.

Pete was killed—crushed—in an accident on his fishing boat. Ever since, I have been haunted by the thought of all that avian information exploding out of his brain—thousands of birds in sudden flight—and wondered where it, and they, have gone. Surely, this pool of knowledge cannot have vaporized. Surely, it has moved on, a flock held together in some inexplicable way, into a habitat where nothing is off-course and nothing could be listed as vagrant or accidental. In one article, Pete wrote: "Someone who delights in observing birds from the kitchen window or from the park bench, but who can identify only a few species, is no less a watcher of birds than the person whose life list numbers in the thousands." *Ave*, Pete.

Choosing a Memory

All day, the color of the grasses changes, and all day, memories flit through the grasses: a crowded crossroads. If I try, I think I see John White, trying to govern an ungovernable population. Then there is Lawson, laboring on, no matter what the impediments, the model of obsession. In a letter of October 30, 1710, he begins by apologizing: "Excuse me not writing sooner wch. was by reason of my too much business." He continues by listing the particulars of the searches he intends.

Of birds, he promises:

> . . . to procure all of this place both land & water fowls from ye Eagle to the wren, to know if possible the age they arrive to, how & where they build their nests, of what material & form, the colour of their eggs and time of their Incubation & flight, their food, beauty & colour, of wt. medicinall uses if any. If rarily designedd to the Life, this would Illustrate such a history very much, their musical notes & cryes must not be omitted, wch. of them abide with us all ye year & those that go away, and wt. strange

birds tempestuous weather winds unusual seasons & other
evidence affords us.
        (Lawson, pp. 270-71)

Surely such obsession, cut short, must live on, an invisible
hunger searching for what it cannot find. If dedication can become obsession, can it swell further into delusion: the whirl-
pool of perception and misperception, hallucination, and mis-
belief? This is where *Fata Morgana* might launch a ship, just over
the horizon, and perhaps upside-down. I wonder if I might not
have been hijacked by someone else's obsessive quest.

In the last golden light of a late afternoon, a single kayaker
paddles his way up the creek in front of our place. As he grows
smaller against the darkening grasses and then disappears from
sight, he could be an Indian of three hundred years ago. He
could be traveling with Lawson or Catesby. The English were
arriving on this coast in ever greater numbers. The terrible
disease that rotted off parts of the body—the English called it
smallpox—was on the loose, traveling from settlement to settlement, killing indiscriminately, pulling off noses. No shaman
could stop it, no matter what his flights or his dances. There
were dark stories being told, disturbing predictions put forth.

In the estuary, all merges, especially at dusk. Boundaries
soften, then collapse—a good place to question what is "real"
and what is not.

At dawn, the landscape comes back gradually. Sometimes, before the terrain is clear, there is a flight of ducks and

sometimes a small band of pelicans cutting through the semi-darkness: the scissors of day cutting away the unseen. Then as light floods over the grasses, revving up the colors from mud to gold, there come flashes of egrets and, this morning, erratic bursts of indistinguishable blackbirds on the far bank of the creek.

I go after my glasses. I look. They are Red-winged Black-birds and, unlike the statue-like Little Egret they surround, they are impatient and staccato. There are about two dozen of them feeding in the cordgrass.

By late in the morning, the Red-winged Blackbirds, the Brown Pelicans, and the Little Egrets have left the creek. A cold wind is blowing. A single male Bufflehead dives and re-emerges over and over as if sewing the creek together. Suddenly, as if to assist, a female and another male join him. The three move slowly up the creek against the tide, a cold and tedious work.

They continue to where the creek forks, choosing the route closer to my shore. They are almost out of sight. They go to join the kayaker and the Indians, the first naturalists and the colonists. But they also stay in my memory. I can call them back at will. At least, for now I can. There were three. It was a cold winter's day. I know it happened and I know that some-where it continues.

Beyond, on the Intracoastal Waterway, a sailboat under power with reefed mainsail appears around a curve and heads towards me. I see a January day with white sail and white-capped ducks on dark blue water: a clear and vivid image. This could be a memory to take into the forever. Perhaps that is how it works: You get only one, as portrayed in the Japanese movie, *Afterlife*—an image of whatever was most beautiful or perfect in your life— and, for those having a hard time remembering, counselors in the life beyond provide a grainy home video of every moment lived. Imagine.

Travel

Travel is a river without name or boundaries. It falls under neither the good god nor the bad god of the Tuscaroras but a demigod slightly higher in a complex, conflicted kingdom. It brings enlightenment and confrontation, appreciation and destruction. It starts with curiosity and does not end, any more than the horizon, which some call God.

It was curiosity that led Lawson to board the ship for Charles Town and curiosity that led him into the wilderness. For Catesby, too, who could easily have found work enough at home, it was curiosity that led him up the unknown rivers of a foreign continent filled with dangers.

And what can be said of John White, who had already ventured with Martin Frobisher to the frozen sea of *Terra Incognita* (now known as Baffin Island) before heading south and west to Roanoke? Was it curiosity that drove him to cross new oceans, or was it personal ambition? And where did he go after he dropped out of recorded history? There are those who say he took one final, fatal trip towards his colony and was buried at sea. We cannot know. We can be certain only that the images of his northern watercolors are so clear that he must have been there with Frobisher on Baffin Island. His art speaks truth.

When American explorer Charles Francis Hall retraced Frobisher's tracks there almost three hundred years later, he was able to do so because of the accuracy of Inuit memory and oral history. The people he questioned, including the centenarian Oo-ki-jox-y Ni-noo, were able to give him surprisingly specific and detailed information which led him to hundreds of pieces of physical evidence ("relics") which he collected and dutifully sent back to England. Frobisher had made three trips—1576, 1577, and 1578. Hall learned that five of Frobisher's men from the first expedition who had gone missing built a boat to escape and, meeting invincible ice, froze to death.

White had been, it is surmised, on the second voyage. But Hall, investigating this history in 1860, did not know to ask for news of an artist, a man who had spent his time while there sketching and painting the inhabitants, a remote people who would hold in their minds memories of these Europeans for hundreds of years. By telling the story over and over they kept that piece of history alive and protected.

What if he had asked for memories of an artist? How much more might we know?

Song at the Edge of Morning

Loneliness hangs over my Carolina marsh. The spirits have turned their backs.

It is a dull overcast morning in mid-January, a time of absolute stillness between first light and the breaking open of day. It might be said that morning has cracked but not yet broken. From far off comes the *caw caw* of crows. There is no breeze and no visible stirring of the water. Strangely, there is no boat traffic out on the river, nor any planes flying from the Marine Air Station. But there is a silent energy at work, a sense of building from within. Color is collecting itself, preparing to rise like a giant regaining consciousness and put itself back together.

Here, at dawn and dusk, it is easy to project over the endless unwalkable acres of watery grass the memories that inhabit us. These memories now wake and stand up. Like kept animals released, they bound out to exercise. They try the limits, they stretch, they experiment with new voices and words. They expand their faces until there is no mistaking them. They assemble and mill together, a parade, a dance, a stroll in the park, an impossible congregation escaped from time and held together only by mind and emotion. The more they run loose, the stronger they become: the stuff of hauntings and specters, those energy patterns that will not break apart unless, somehow, released and given rest. They might also be mirages, reflections of glaciers or of people walking about in some town many miles away below the horizon—people who would be very surprised to know how they were being observed from afar—as a *Fata Morgana*.

The abiding question remains: Do apparitions come from outside of us or inside? Do they come from "another world" or from energy patterns deeply rooted in this world and ourselves? While Buddhists and proponents of Unidentified Flying Objects argue the particulars, I keep looking out over the marsh, trying to focus.

I see my brother, born a year ahead of me, so close in age and looks we were often mistaken for twins. We could have stayed close in adult life but did not. In spite of certain common interests, especially those of a metaphysical nature, we grew apart. He stopped answering his phone. He taught French and Latin at a country day school, but we knew little else of his life. When he traveled to Ireland, he visited Sligo and the grave of the poet William Butler Yeats. Knowing I would be pleased, he sent me a photo of the tombstone with the epitaph: "Cast a cold Eye/On Life, on Death./Horseman, pass by." That was before the late night angry phone calls and the wild accusations.

My reverie breaks as suddenly a single duck flies up from a watery edge and wobbles across the sky: perhaps the shears that morning needed to cut itself from night.

What follows this unidentifiable duck? A greater depth of color, though still not risen from its bed; a spilling out of that color from the grass into the creek; a first pelican of the day flying low over the water along the opposite bank; a gull; then, high overhead, the same duck, looping back as if having gained altitude and set its course.

When I concentrate and watch these birds, I do not see the faces in the marsh and wonder of their origins and suffer again the loss of those I loved. And so I come to understand that watching birds, even if I am only beginning to learn to focus, is a meditation that takes me out of myself and dissipates my hauntings and obsessions. If, as has been said, singing hymns is praying twice, then watching birds is achieving the silence and peace of grace. It brings you to a place of calm within the center of yourself from where you can pivot in all directions, or no direction.

Minutes later, the egrets have returned to the grassy wilderness that spreads before me and do their peculiar dance before settling down to feed. I know now that morning has broken.

Because I never know how blackbird will speak to me and which of its many forms it will assume, I must watch and listen carefully: one of the lessons of blackbird.

Blackbird as Pirate

Be careful with memory. Its contents are not necessarily facts, but impressions, symbols, poems, and brushstrokes. It isn't a machine with an "On" button.

Just as you cannot trust memory, you cannot trust what you think you know. A species you think you have identified can easily disguise itself and confuse you as you struggle to verify it. Consider the Red-winged Blackbird:

The male carries the colors of a pirate flag: red for blood (and for no mercy) and black for death. It flashes that flag as a sign of aggression and a means of establishing territory that will be inviting to a female, not to attract the female to itself. A male Red-winged Blackbird consciously uses his epaulets to warn off other males, or not, depending on his assertiveness and relationship to others in the flock. He attracts females by the territory he controls, not the color he displays.

Pirates were well aware of the psychology of color. The "black spot," a death threat, inspired the utmost terror.

Pirates would dress for battle, just as warring Native Americans would. A ring of color around an eye, a ring of metal in the ear, feathers, bandannas, a cutlass, multiple pistols, burning pine pitch, smoke in the beard: The uniform of fear could greatly increase effectiveness, as could songs, chants, and ghoulish dances.

Sometimes it is difficult to distinguish just what kind of blackbird you are looking at, especially when they mingle in large winter flocks: one of the blackbirds bearing color; or one not bearing color: a female bird or an immature one. Are they pests or not? And so with pirates, who often commanded high social favor in the new colonies and traveled with a variety of species. Friend or foe? Hero or anti-hero? Sometimes it was a matter as simple as a shift in politics abroad or personal favor with a monarch. A "letter of marque and reprisal," the license for a privateer, made plunder a job description and piracy a monarch's order.

Pirate, privateer, buccaneer, corsair, adventurer, soldier, sailor, mutineer, militia, raider, slaver: The titles, nationalities, allegiances, and activities of sea adventurers are confused with time, crossed purposes, and myth. Many buccaneers like Henry Morgan ("The Pirate King") or pirates like Edward Teach, who developed the hellish persona of "Blackbeard," complete with burning fuses in his beard, became far larger than life, an emblem of terror and the stuff of fiction. Others, petty criminals, simply made a living out of seizing what was available along an unprotected and lawless coastline out of the reach of the Royal Navy. All were violent, greedy, opportunistic, and all were dependent upon islands. Only nature could control these marine robbers. Hurricanes forced them to migrate, but this meant simply changing their geographical focus on a seasonal basis.

The Carolina coast was perfect for their purposes and became nursery, staging area, and launch pad for terror at sea.
Except for the incalculable hazard of storms and mosquito-
borne illnesses, the coast provided everything that was necessary: proximity to the Caribbean with its Spanish riches and
growing trade in slaves, rum, and sugar; an undefended and
sparse populace, as well as one that often needed protection
from attacking Indians and was willing to pay; temperate climate; and a roiling political situation mixing Spanish, French,
English, and Native American power plays an ocean away
from the control of home armies. Here, in this feverish brew,
the "Brethren of the Coast" flourished and held sway for decades—from 1650 to 1725: a maritime mafia with its precise
code of ethics and its uniforms of fear.

Blackbirds will kill other birds; blackbirds will do whatever
they have to do—change range or diet and take many mates—
in order to survive. They have strong, straight bills with sharp
tips and the ability to open their mouths wide to bore into a
surface for food unavailable to other avian families. A Red-
winged Blackbird, though smaller than an American Robin,
will take on a hawk.

I have no memory or knowledge of ancestors as pirates but
know we are all capable of deceit. My brother died at age 63
from the results of a fall down the stairs in his house. Whether
or not he was pushed by his partner cannot be known, but the
partner did not seek medical help for some days, in spite of
entreaties by the neighbors. The improvident partner inher-
ited my brother's estate, which still provides a livelihood for

him and his mother. We were left with Annabelle, an African Grey Parrot who had pulled out most of her feathers and who would need a home for many years.

A Red-winged Blackbird is the only bird that has attacked me, flying at my head when I ventured too close to his territory on a golf fairway along a marshy creek bed. The only other bird attack I have experienced is a Spotted Towhee who once spent three days pecking at his reflection in a large window in our house until we realized what he was doing and drew the shades to remove his imaginary competitor. Under attack from the blackbird, I retreated.

I think of all those who fell before Blackbeard, even the guardians of the city of Charleston, which he managed to blockade for a week in 1718.

I think of all the farmers, backed by the U. S. Department of Agriculture, who have fought off blackbird invaders with pesticides, the plots that have been hatched to kill millions of birds hungry to feed on crops of sunflower seeds and wheat. Sometimes caged Red-winged Blackbirds were used as decoys to attract wild ones to a poisoned area, reminiscent of how pirates at times would switch flags to decoy a victim ship.

Today, the pirates are gone, at least the "Brethren of the Coast" with their cruel acts of enslavement and marooning, and so are most of the lethal plans of federal agricultural managers. Blackbird persists. I am glad to have felt its wings in my hair, that beating flash of red across my forehead, a reminder of what might be—a collision with beauty, a collision with terror. It is hard to know the difference.

Blackbird: Its Silence on a Winter's Day

Winter is a kind of silence: blanks on a map or empty spaces in documentation, a place where pages have been ripped out by blizzard or by desperate hands. It is the time, Catesby frequently noted, when "birds of passage" are absent.

This morning a fierce wind is blowing from the northwest. Overnight, a large storm system passed by to the east, a sweep of ice and snow from the plains across the mid-Atlantic and on up into New England. The coldest weekend of the winter is forecast.

Once, as Lawson traveled, a "violent" wind from the northwest threatened to blow down the Sapona village where he was staying until the chief ran out into the gale and, addressing it, calmed it in "two minutes." It was the *Devil*, the chief said, angry because the village had not put to death a group of prisoners they had recently released. The native people, Lawson noted, were accurate in how they named the winds:

> *Besides, they have Names for eight of the thirty two points, and call the Winds by their several Names, as we do; but indeed more properly, for the North-West Wind is called*

*the cold Wind; the North-East the wet Wind; the South
the warm Wind, and so agreeably of the rest.*
(Lawson, p. 213)

Long after first light, there is no sign of bird life except for a single crow riding the updrafts and, far in the distance, one gull careening wildly on different currents: black and white, daring the wind. No planes, no boats. The river is moving, but blackbird is not flying.

Then suddenly, as the cordgrass catches fire with sunlight, blackbird *is* flying: a wave of red-flagged wings sweeping unevenly out into the marsh. Simultaneously, a barge with crane pushed by a tug enters the river and a plane takes off from the Marine Air Station. A new page of deep blue water etched with white script is set forth for translation and revision.

The tide is halfway to high. What there is to concentrate on now is the shining slivers of ice on the marsh grass below me: winter rubrics. By noon they will have disappeared, leaving no directions, no clues.

Blackbird: Taking the Place of Moon

The moon, a perfect sphere, is riding above the colors of dawn. I put the binoculars on it and examine its topography—the shaded areas that could be continents, the empty areas once thought to be seas. Though few have visited, many have named these fabled parts, and some of these names roll through me: Mare Frigoris, Mare Imbrium, Mare Serenitatis. In the southwest quadrant, where perhaps Australia should be, an enormous crater. I can almost see Canada, almost the United States.

I look for what Harriot might have seen. Just ahead of Galileo, he was the first to make a telescopic drawing of the moon, breaking the news of its mountains. (He was also the first to draw sunspots.) I squint, trying to see what he saw through his six-powered telescope. If I knew where to look, I might find the crater named for him at Lat. 33.1N, Long. 114.3E. Here, he is finally gathered together, come home, to the moon.

After all the adventures of his life and beyond—his bones and monument were destroyed in the Great Fire of London in 1666—Harriot is remembered for his algebra. "Algebra" derives from Italian, Spanish, Latin, and Arabic words meaning "reunion of broken parts." Maybe "algebra" is our final word, or the clue that points the way. Perhaps it is as important as "Croatoan," the last hope for the lost colonists. But too much can be made of words and their influence. I remember John White's last ship which got him nowhere was named the *Hopewell*.

I am brought back quickly to the marsh. A tremulous flight of blackbirds has just sung its way out over the creek. I am reeled in to here and now, birdsong and tide: the foreground of another cold January day on the South Carolina coast. As I concentrate on what is in front of me, the moon slowly rolls towards the pastel atmosphere which will erode, disfigure, and consume it, until all that remains lives in my mind. A plane flies over the moon and a tern beneath it. The moon, as it disappears, takes everything with it, including the tern. No wonder it was thought by some that "birds of passage" fly to the moon in winter.

Suddenly, along the far bank, I see something different: a moving dark shape that is not a bird. As I watch, it slips out from the grass into the water: a Land (or River) Otter. It swims first one way, north up the creek, then turns and swims about a hundred yards in the other direction, dives, and disappears. It is hunting. Somewhere, in the acres and acres of watery grass, it makes its home.

Otter: Watching from the Edge

The otter was one of Lawson's "Beasts of Carolina" and one of the animals, he suggested, that the Indians might keep and give as a gift under the general appellation of "slave." It is hard to imagine the otter as captive, though James I is said to have had a pack of tame otters that fished for him. They were managed by their own "Keeper of the King's Otters."

Otters are unusually intelligent animals and among the few species which engage in organized play. I have watched them on a dock, tossing a fish back and forth, reveling in pattern and precision.

According to the Tlingits of Southeast Alaska, Kooshdaka, or the spirit of Land Otter, is a transformational being that haunts the mountainous, forested coast, listening for the calls of those lost in the woods or at sea. Practicing an enmity of long duration, the spirit captures human beings to avenge their killing of otters. Adept at changing shape, Kooshdaka will take the form of people known to the victim and offer rescue. If it succeeds in transporting the victim to its own shadowy home underground where all otters can appear as humans and the dwelling as the victim's own home, only a shaman can retrieve the unwitting guest. If not reclaimed, the prisoner becomes a Land Otter, unable to return to his own people. With his soul stolen, the shell of his human form remains, wandering vacantly in the place where he became lost.

Kooshdaka searches especially for vulnerable children. If a child strays into the woods while picking berries, for instance, Kooshdaka might appear as a parent or close relative, imitating familiar voices, and entice the child to follow.

Kooshdaka, ever present, waiting and listening on the edge, watches for canoes in distress, for disoriented hunters, hikers, and those caught unaware in the stormy and foggy coastlands.

Not simply local myth, Kooshdaka sightings and stories occur insistently. Anthropologist Frederica de Laguna, famed for her work among the Tlingit of Southeast Alaska, stated, "Everyone, myself included, has had some personal experience of a sudden or startling encounter with a land otter."

I had heard tales of Kooshdaka leaping on a moving car and of a person, long missing, found on a beach, her torn fingernails tearing at shells as she stared emptily out to sea, but my daughter Helen, aged nine, was the first in our family to encounter Land Otter.

It was the evening of the Fourth of July at our house in Juneau. She had gone out to the back yard to feed her rabbits, Frank and Kermit. Suddenly Kooshdaka appeared in front of her, only inches away, rearing up on his hind legs taller than she. He did not peer into her eyes but electrified her with his strength. He was gone before she had come out of a momentary paralysis. Helen describes this meeting as a "column of pure power—shiny brown." The awe stays with her.

Traveling in the Dead of Winter

John Lawson set out in the dead of winter, pursuing a course so difficult and twisted he thought it twice as long as it was. (He called his account of the expedition his "1,000 Mile Journal.") No wonder. Rivers overflowed with swollen tributaries; the Santee was up 36 feet. Creeks wound like labyrinths through the marshes, rising and falling with the tide, while a canoe-eating current snaked through the flood. Only Sewee guides in their small canoes could manage, but one of Lawson's was drunk and there wasn't always room in the fragile vessels for all the party.

During one such instance not far into the journey, Lawson and his companions fell into a creek they were trying to cross with a pole. All the bedding was soaked and soon frozen with wind from the northwest. After a wretched night "that I never desire to have the like again," they were saved in the morning by a "large Fire of the *Indians*," but not for long. Later that day, they had to strip off their clothes and wade through a swamp tangled by fallen trees. When they got to the hut of Scipio, an absent hunter, they made themselves at home as was the custom. With the bitter northwest wind still pursuing them, they settled in to cook and warm themselves but managed to set the roof on fire.

Lawson died at the hands of the Tuscaroras in September 1711. He met his end almost by coincidence, just as he had set out for the colonies almost by coincidence.

What Lawson did not know, when he planned his 1711 trip up the Neuse River, was that the Indian tribes of North Carolina had secretly plotted to attack the settlers of Bath County at dawn on September 22, 1711. Their goal was annihilation of the white presence that had exploited, insulted, and enslaved them. Debt, drunkenness, and disease had taken too large a toll on their good will, and there could be no turning back. It was an irrevocable date. When Lawson and his associate Christopher Von Graffenried set off on approximately September 12, they were headed into a certain fate. They were quickly captured and Lawson killed.

It was several days after the death of Lawson that 500 Indians gathered at the village of Catechna, then fanned out in small groups among the settlements along the Neuse, Pamlico, and Trent rivers to position themselves to consummate the plot. Considered friends, they aroused no suspicion as they mingled among the colonists. At dawn on Saturday, September 22, they burst out in war paint, their eyes circled, to massacre and defile men, women, and children. They pillaged the houses and destroyed the crops, leaving behind horrendous scenes and brutal vignettes, as described by Von Graffenreid: "Pregnant women had the unborn children ripped out and hung upon trees." By the end of the rampage, approximately 140 settlers were dead, 30 taken prisoner—to serve as slaves—and many left wounded. Lawson's town of Bath was now a refugee center, holding over 300 widows and orphans.

The first real help came from South Carolina, in the person of John Barnwell, founder of Beaufort, commissioned by the Charles Town Assembly to lead a charge in aid of their neighbors to the north. His force was composed of 33 whites on horseback and 495 Indians of allied tribes. They reached the Neuse River on January 29, 1712, and Bath on February 10. During April they lay siege to the fort of the local potentate, Chief Hancock. The campaign, which earned Barnwell the name "Tuscarora Jack," lasted all winter but brought no peace.

The Yemasee and Other Wars

By 1715, John White and Thomas Harriot had long since fallen off the map, while John Lawson's shadow lingered. In Amsterdam, Maria Sibylla Merian, the magician of metamorphosis, who had continued, somehow, to pull brilliant colors out of poverty and illness, now suffered a stroke. She would linger for two more years.

Of my naturalist-guides, only Mark Catesby was still active in the southeastern colonies, traveling, observing, collecting, negotiating with his patrons, painting, and writing (while making liberal use of Lawson's work and learning from Merian's style).

The Carolina coast had become a never-ending battlefield. The war with the Tuscarora had recently ended, and now the Yemassee, aided by the Creeks and others, erupted. Blackbeard, merchant of terror, flourished. Fear bred in the marshes. Up and down the coast, pirates foraged in that fear and found good living. Even after the pirates were quelled, foreboding would persist: Raids by pistol or hatchet still threatened. Settlers could be kidnapped, enslaved, tortured, or hacked apart at any time by any number of potential enemies, often in league with one another. Raising the level of terror, mythic figures floated through the watery coastline. When Blackbeard was locked in final battle in North Carolina's Ocracoke Inlet with two armed sloops, it is said he was wounded more than twenty-five times and that, after the final blow, his beheaded body swam several times around the sloop that took him. The wraith of the "devil incarnate," as he wanted to be known, is said to haunt certain beaches even today, along with the shades of his victims.

The Revolutionary War brought little improvement. Treachery came under many guises. In 1779, as the British retreated south from Charleston to Beaufort through the twisting coastal waterways, they found themselves encumbered by Native American satellites and thousands of escaped slaves. As these would-be-helpers and mendicants clung to their boats, the British cut off their fingers and finally abandoned them to starvation and fever on Otter Island in St. Helena Sound. Sir Francis Drake, warrior-pirate, had done the same in 1586 when he abandoned Indian and African slaves on the Outer Banks after evacuating the desperate Roanoke settlers.

It was only after the Revolution that conditions in the Beaufort area began to improve, and that was only because of a change of crop. Sea cotton, considered the finest form of cotton, now replaced indigo, which, in turn, had replaced rice. The profitable new agriculture vastly increased the fortunes of certain leading families such as the Barnwells. It also required the importation of large numbers of African slaves.

The rush of new slaves, mostly from what is now Congo, Angola, and Sierra Leone, into the isolated Sea Islands resulted in a concentration of culture which has lasted to this day: Gullah has woven a folklore rich with boodaddies (spirits of witch doctors), drolls (spirits of young children who died a painful death), hags, and haints.

Hags are witches who travel by night, giving nightmares to their victims. Haints, or haunts, are spirits of the dead which can appear anywhere but which prefer graveyards and swamps, especially in the full of the moon. Haints are spirits caught between this world and the next, spirits you do not want to confront, and so you paint your porch ceilings and your shutters "haint" blue to keep them away.

In the prosperous, relatively quiet time between wars, Beaufort plantation owner and state senator William Elliott (1788-1863) spent much time hunting. Fortunately for us, he recorded some of his experiences, providing glimpses of a way of life about to shatter. Not only was the plantation economy soon to collapse; already, as he comments, the local wildlife was changing.

Elliott starts his book, *Carolina Sports by Land and Water*, with an energetic salutation to Frenchman Jean Ribaut, who attempted to settle Port Royal in 1562. It was, he imagines, a glorious scene that greeted this early visitor, a wildly abundant garden where "herds of deer and buffalo browsed, unconscious of fear, on the luxuriant herbage—and birds of unknown plumage and unrivalled voice, fluttered and carolled among the trees." (Elliott, p. 13)

Towards the end of the book, Elliott tells us that the panther and the wolf are "now nearly extinct," as well as the buffalo, which, as Catesby informs us in 1712, was found "in herds within thirty miles of Charleston." (p. 232)

Elliott offers the reasons: the swamps drained for rice cultivation and the forests cleared for corn and cotton. The crops dependent on slaves were weakening the soil, unraveling the ecosystem, and threatening the economy. It was this very deterioration that enabled Elliott to hunt over his vast estates, a total of twelve plantations. Elliott expresses a foreboding but manifests paralysis. He might be called one of America's earliest environmentalists, but one incapable of taking action. Educated and aware, Elliott was nonetheless bound by the slave-economy that maintained his life style and held him in thrall.

Interested in local culture, Elliott provides one tale redolent of the marsh and its mysteries. After a fabulous day of hunting at his Chee-Ha Plantation, a day of bears shot and a wounded deer gone inexplicably missing——the situation reminded Elliott of the story of the "Spectre Buck":

A malcontent by the name of May who had lived nearby ordered his slaves on his death to bury him at midnight without ceremony in a shallow, hidden grave in the wilds. They followed his orders. Ever after, "The negro looks on this as haunted ground," sometimes experiencing hot air rushing from the site of the grave which causes a cold shivering, and sometimes "a milk-white buck is seen, by glimpses of the moon, taking gigantic leaps—then shrouded in a mist wreath, and changed, in a twinkling, into the likeness of a pale old

man, swathed in his grave clothes—then melting away slowly
into air!" (pp. 206-207)

Significantly, Elliott then launches into a discussion of hal-
lucinations resulting from fever and quinine: a danger endemic
in the lowcountry. Malaria was the great leveler along the coast.
Everyone lived in fear of it, planter and slave. It did not always
kill but led to chronic debilitating weakness and susceptibility
to infection and other diseases. The visions it spawned—Elliott referred to them as *phantasmagoria*, "a shadowy proces-
sion"—hung over the marshes, especially during the months
from August to December when its accompanying fevers and
chills came out of hiding in the bloodstream and wracked the
victim's body. This was the time and domain of hallucination.

Deep down, Elliott knew the fate that was catching up
with the South. He saved his last words, however, for the protection of game: "So that we may yet hope to see the time
when men may, under the sanction of the law, and without
offence, or imputation of aristocracy, preserve the game from
extermination—and perpetuate, in so doing, the healthful,
generous, and noble diversion of hunting." (p. 260)

When the end came to the cotton kingdom of Beaufort,
it came almost as quickly as an Indian raid. Beaufort fell without a fight on November 7, 1861, when a large Union naval
force overwhelmed the small Confederate presence. But it did
not come without warning. The previous Saturday, the town
received word that an invincible Union force was on its way,
and Beaufort began to pack up. On Sunday, Reverend Joseph
Walker, pastor of St. Helena's Episcopal Church, announced

he would have the church bells rung the next day at noon, reminding all to pray. But his congregation was already preparing
to leave—for their plantations upcountry or, if the plantations
were considered "unsafe for ladies," for Charleston. Tradition
has it that by the time the Union soldiers arrived, only one
man, a drunk Irishman, was found in the streets—and thus the
town was spared. Union forces quickly transformed it into a
hospital base and regional headquarters which they maintained
throughout the war. Churches as well as houses were used as
hospitals, and operations were performed on tombstones bor-
rowed from the burial grounds.

On the eve of flight, Emily Barnwell Walker, 15, recalled:

> *That evening I went to church alone. A little bird flew in
> and round and round it went. I was feeling bad before; that
> almost put an end to my self control.*
>
> (Barnwell, *The Story of an American Family*, p.
> 190)

Beaufort Vanquished, the Barnwells in Diaspora

The Emancipation Proclamation was read on January 1, 1863, at Camp Saxton, former plantation of John Joyner Smith, in the town of Port Royal, just south of Beaufort.

A former slave, remembering the time, said, "Freedom came and was like having gone to the Devil and come back." (*Voices of Carolina Slave Children*, p. 47) I think this former slave was saying his new situation might have been like heaven, but it took the newly freed slaves only so far.

Afterwards, the 1st South Carolina Volunteers, the first federally authorized African-American regiment formed during the Civil War, received its national and regimental colors. Its colonel was Thomas Wentworth Higginson, northern abolitionist and literary guide of Emily Dickinson.

Soon after, Higginson would lead his troops on campaign into Florida and then Georgia. And, as he traveled with his men, he collected African-American spirituals: "Often in the starlit evening," he wrote, he would return to camp "from some lonely ride by a swift river, or on the plover-haunted barrens" to find his men singing and dancing. Surreptitiously, he would write down the words of the song and carry the transcription to his tent "like some captured bird or insect." All the many songs he recorded, Higginson asserts, were "a stimulus to courage and a tie to heaven." (*Atlantic Monthly,* June, 1867)

There was less singing among the white population. After the war, if former landowners returned to Beaufort, they found they no longer belonged. General Stephen Elliott, visiting his plantation on Parris Island, was treated with great respect and affection by his former slaves but firmly told, "We own this land now." (Barnwell, p. 219) There was no compensation for confiscated property and little opportunity to buy it back. Not only had Reconstruction come to the South; so did the Panic of 1873, which festered into the global "Long Depression" of 1873-79. Former plantation owners and their families had to go where a living could be found. For some, that was New York.

Edward King, an Englishman visiting the south in 1873, noted of Beaufort that it was beautiful:

> *But the silence of the grave reigned everywhere. Many of the mansions were closed or fallen into decay....A wealthy and highly prosperous community had been reduced to beggary.*
> (Barnwell, p. 219)

The Barnwells, descendants of "wild goose" John (Tuscarora Jack) Barnwell of Ireland—a founder, patriarch, and leading citizen of Beaufort—had been dislodged. Like a flock of blackbirds shocked from a tree, they were on the move and in need of new territory. In diaspora, they would take to all parts of the country. Although their blood would continue in Beaufort through intermarriage, the name would fade, except in the burial ground at St. Helena's Episcopal Church. (Today, a small number of Barnwell listings can be found out of thousands in the regional phone book; one, my neighbor, is African-American.)

When he died in 1724, John Barnwell left a large family and an estate of 6,500 acres as well as a distinguished record as colonial administrator, diplomat, and soldier. His prolific and energetic family continued to amass property and influence while maintaining his standard for leadership. But today his progeny, scattered geographically, would be hard to identify individually. Their genealogist and historian, Stephen B. Barnwell, titled their chronicle *The Story of an American Family*. It was the story of blackbird, the story of all of us.

Like the Barnwells, my family had emigrated from the Old to the New World, had established a social position, made and lost fortunes, held to a specific geographic area—in our case, New York—achieved a comfortable reputation and status, then weakened and scattered.

Now, I had traveled further than most of them. "Coming out" parties and elite clubs were a thing of the past. I had gone to the north, to make a life in Alaska where opportunities abounded. I had gone to the south, to escape the cold in winter. I now reversed my ancestors' course: I traveled to Ireland as a tourist. I made two trips, one with friends to the Yeats festival held each summer in Sligo and one with my family on a horseback riding tour of the western coast. I stood in front of Yeats's gravestone and read his enigmatic words for myself.

Making a Life List

There are many ways to keep a list of birds. You might maintain a checklist or make notes in a field guide, marking your sightings with dates and particulars. You might keep different lists for different times and regions. You might keep lists of birds you have encountered in books or songs or, like Roger Tory Peterson, those you see or hear in movies. New cell phone applications now make it possible to pursue and find species wherever you are—and grow your lists more quickly and easily than ever before.

But all the time, no matter what your method—old-fashioned or new—you are building a Life List. This is the record that leads you forward. This is the record that also takes you back—a trail of feathers marking the course you have chosen. This is your expedition log, your memory. You left the kitchen window, opened the porch door, hesitated, then walked down the steps, crossed the lawn, alone. Then you went on, beyond what you knew, finding yourself without guidance. Perhaps you lost your log. The surf came up. The canoe capsized. You had to make a hurried escape—from enemies, disease, poverty, a hurricane. You came back with only your memories and no specimens for your patrons.

They were angrily disappointed. But each memory is alive, whether you can recall it or not. You watched the bird and the bird happened; it flies yet just above the marsh, the child of Eros and Chaos. And as you travel forward, each bird comes with you, opening up a new channel with new opportunities to see and hear. Each checkmark is a step that can never be erased: a bridge that carries you across the marsh of the in-between to the unknown lands beyond. Remember, nothing happens until you look.

The Family Icteridae comes towards the end of the ornithological list. You go through columns and columns of birds before you come to the kinship of Bobolink, Meadowlark, Blackbird, Grackle, Cowbird, and Oriole. Only the Finches and their allies (Fringillidae) and Old World Sparrows (Passeridae) follow. Of course, as with most of life, you jump around. You would not start with Common Loon and work your way through the species until you came to House Sparrow, not unless you were pathologically obsessed. At that point, you probably would not be able to care about the birds you saw or be able to create an image to carry away. You would be lost in the list, blinded by order and task. You would not be able to *see the bird.*

Sometimes it is easy to overlook what seems to be invisible. You might be carried away by pelicans or hawks and not notice the Common Grackle. You might forget to look at yourself and your family and the small flights which make up your life, the thousands of wings which brought you here, faithfully beating across oceans and mountains.

Think of the magic of small everyday acts: your forebears getting up in the morning and entering a forest to chop wood or walking down dusty paths to obtain water, attend school, work a job, raise a family—all that doing and loving and loss to make the way possible for you, their unseen hope.

Think of the magic of opening the door each day and finding morning there, dressed in gypsy clothes. How far has she traveled to find you? How many wings have exhausted themselves to give you life and bear you up?

Sometimes those wings have darkened the sky; sometimes they have thinned to a shadow, but always they are flitting over the marsh, stretching, rising, and falling, reminding you how you came to be here. The air is thick with their beating. You might not recognize the species. It might have no name: all the more reason to go in pursuit and report back—to "counterfeit the truth."

This is where blackbird, having flown north to claim a new territory, flies off the map. Here is the land of the unknown, where you must go on alone, just as John Lawson did, and Catesby. Here is where the garden gate swings shut behind you—a sound you cannot forget. There is no turning back—and, you fully realize, you are alone.

The early itinerant naturalists did not always know what they were looking at and sometimes had to make guesses or simply describe what they saw as best they could. An example is the European mavis. The species of thrush, or mavis, that Catesby saw in America and described has never been determined. He called it the "Little Thrush." It never sings, he says, "having only a single note. ... They are seldom seen, being but few, and those abiding only in dark recesses of the thickest woods and swamps. Their food is the berries of holly, haws, etc." He depicted his thrush almost hidden in the branches of dahoon holly, known as Christmas berry. (Catesby, p.101)

I might think of my mother as a little thrush in a large city, hidden away and not able to be identified by sight or sound, but comfortable in her setting as long as it stayed secure. I wanted her to be protected.

But I could not offer security. I had learned that over and over from my three guides.

My mother spent much time in her later years sitting on the couch in the living room of her small co-op apartment. She had fought her way back from alcoholism but had lost her marriage and lovely eighteenth century house where ghosts stirred.

The coffee table in front of her living room couch now stands before my living room couch on the other side of the country. In dark colors it bears an image of a two-masted schooner. This could be the *Flying Dutchman*, the phantom ship condemned to circle the earth forever. Or it could simply be an amateurish depiction of a generic vessel, made more valuable, the assessor of her estate noted, because of its "distressed" surface.

In her last years my mother, living alone, had a good friend named "Edith." They often went to movies together. When Edith died, my mother drifted into a decline. I don't think she ever went to another movie, though they played continuously only a few blocks away. She had television. Her favorite programs were English comedy, golf, and weather. Like a bird dependent on atmospheric conditions, she followed the reports of wind and wave carefully.

Treasures of a Grandmother's House

Sometimes, memory opens with a book and starts with "once upon a time."

When Nabokov, famed for his memory, was about eight, he discovered in the attic of his family's country house fifty miles from St. Petersburg a hidden treasure: a stash of books that had belonged to his maternal grandmother, who had been interested in natural history. These "glorious loads of fantastically attractive volumes" included "Maria Sibylla Merian's lovely plates of Surinam insects." I think of the child writer-to-be poring over these books with a surge of delight.

I remember sitting in an alcove between two living rooms in my paternal grandmother's house in Walpole, New Hampshire, discovering English children's books with wonderful illustrations. One was *Blackie's Children's Annual*, first published in 1904. The room facing south was informal, a sitting room; the other was formal, a salon with walls displaying the "Monuments of Paris" wallpaper by Joseph Dufour hand painted many generations before and miraculously preserved through all the harsh New Hampshire winters weathered by the house. (Temperatures had been recorded in pencil on another hand-painted wallpaper in the hallway by the seldom-used north door.) Just outside the wall that joined these two rooms was a row of lilac bushes grown tall as trees. It was here, it is said, that Louisa May Alcott wrote *Under the Lilacs*, and it was here that I played, and read, as a child.

The "Knapp House," as it was known, was considered the best example of 1812 architecture in the country, with secret hiding places in preparation for attack by the British and a "widow's walk" on the roof which looked out not to sea but to fields of grass woven with Queen Anne's Lace and Black-eyed Susans. Sometimes my grandmother, Agnes Cantine Bunker, would hide things in the secret places (a false stair, a revolving wall in the library) before leaving the house for the winter and then not be able to remember where she had hidden them.

It is here that memory, for me, begins to take shape: whole scenes, like the wallpaper in the drawing room, in which one item, one person connects with another—the house on its hilltop, the village at its feet, the Connecticut River Valley winding below with the trill of church bells and the whistle of a distant train.

It was here I heard my first ghost story: My grandparents and my great aunt and uncle Parsons were sitting on the summer lawn in front of the house after dinner when a young woman in white, skimming above the ground, raced up to them begging for help, then vanished before they could get up to assist her. The next morning, they heard that a young woman had been murdered at that time down by the tracks in the village.

There was another village. In the middle of the dining room table where we gathered three times a day, sat a Spode tureen in the Blue Willow pattern. Its painted decoration alluded to the story of the two lovers who, pursued and separated in life, found eternal union when they died and the gods took pity on them, transforming them into swallows flying forever across a china sky.

Swallows eat and drink in flight, swooping through air to catch flying insects. Catesby's "American Swallow," as he called it, is the Chimney Swift. Such "birds of passage," he hypothesized, "pass to the same latitude in the Southern Hemisphere, as the northern latitude whence they came."

Stories, lovers, and lilacs: How interwoven memory is; how mercurial and strange.

And Louisa May Alcott—What of her?

Her story opens: "The elm-tree avenue was all overgrown, the great gate was never unlocked. ... Yet voices were heard about the place, the lilacs nodded over the high wall as if they said, 'We could tell fine secrets if we chose.'"

By the time I became conscious of the place, Dutch Elm Disease had destroyed the tree avenue, but the lilacs were still there and undoubtedly the secrets as well. Alcott's story ends with the lines: "The long-closed gate opens and the path to the house becomes free to all comers for a hospitable welcome. ... Under the Lilacs."

I like to think I am still on that path, the door to the house wide open; but I am not sure. Long after we had left Walpole, we learned through a mutual acquaintance that the new owners would like to hear some of the history of the place. I wrote to them, providing information I thought they would like to have. I never heard back. And now that information floats somewhere, orphaned and unclaimed.

Memory, Collecting and Choosing

The itinerant naturalist-explorers all shared a common dilemma: They had to decide not only what to write down or sketch but also what to collect and bring back out of the wilderness. The European mania for collecting was obsessive but paid well and underwrote voyages of discovery, and their patrons were often not only specific but demanding. Sometimes what these patrons wanted was different from what the naturalists wanted. Sometimes hard-won items had to be left behind, either because of logistics or exigencies. There were losses and long delays, and sometimes there were thefts. When specimens were packed in rum or other spirits, the temptation for thirsty sailors could become too great.

When Drake forced the hurried evacuation of Roanoke colony in 1586, trunks of Harriot's seeds and specimens were lost in the surf, and some, though fortunately not all, of John White's maps and watercolors. Frobisher was perhaps watching as White's papers drowned in the evacuation, remembering what had been lost before in the frozen sea of *Terra Incognita* during his trips of the 1570's. How many of the artist's sketches and paintings of Inuit life on Baffin Island had already disappeared, and under what conditions, we can only wonder—as with the remaining chapters of the artist's life.

For Harriot, too, there was a pattern set. His papers would scatter like seeds on the waves, his algebraic formulas like twisting underwater grasses. His *Briefe and True Report* was his only title to be published during his lifetime, and what it was, not surprisingly for the times, was an advertising pamphlet. His employer, Ralegh, subcontractor to Queen Elizabeth I, was in the business of establishing colonies. Harriot's job was to attract prospective colonists by extolling the qualities of the new-found lands; happily for him, he had many from which to choose.

When I think of my portfolio of memories, I wonder which I should try to save in a rising surf. There was the house in Walpole, but there were other houses as well, such as my maternal grandmother's house in Water Mill, built partly of ship's timbers washed ashore. There were people and pets, stories strange and wonderful, and scenes I wish I could forget. What good would it do to salvage just a few memories without context?

When my mother died, what was left of her memories and stories went with her; already dementia had robbed her of most. I have certain fragments she left with me—childhood stories, such as the time she rushed home after a summer's absence to tug at a closet door being held closed by a robber inside the closet; a French governess named M'amselle; a smooth-haired fox terrier named Happy; riding out the Hurricane of 1938 in Southampton (a neighbor's hair turned white overnight as he clung to a floating door); a bicycle trip through Europe on the eve of the Second World War, sleeping in hay stacks while the Nazi shadow lengthened. Should I try to re-play these memories, though I have no grainy home video, and then describe them and classify them? Are they of importance to anyone but her? Might they have been returned to her when she died?

What happens to memory when it breaks loose and flies off on its own? Does it fall like shards of pottery in what was once John White's village, leaving clues but no answer?

As I wonder, sitting here on my Carolina ledge, something hovers over the marsh, but I cannot name it and know no Linnaeus of the nonphysical to consult. I travel towards it but cannot reach it: a wavering and luminous flight of faces and scenes, a *phantasmagoria* such as William Elliott described. It re-minds me of what passed before my sleeping eyes when I was taking the anti-malarial drug Larium while traveling in Africa: huge long parades of contorted faces; and always, that of my mother, who was still alive at the time.

I Meet Robert Louis Stevenson

Another day passes with its choices: now, at low tide, mid-afternoon, two Great Blue Heron; two Great Egret; a tern; a crow; the regular two pairs of Bufflehead who visit often; and then a sweep of crows, surrounding my field of vision, calling.

I remember something more.

I am eight years old and in my grandmother's bedroom in her apartment at 1088 Park Avenue. It is a large apartment in the large building built by her father, Robert J. Cuddihy, publisher of *The Literary Digest* and America's first pollster.

Her room, as I remember it, is decorated in pink and peach and cream. I am lying in her large bed with monogrammed sheets and delicate lace and satin coverings. Even as an eight-year-old accustomed to comfortable surroundings, I know I am lying in luxury. I am recovering from a tonsillectomy (customary in those days) and my grandmother is reading to me. She is reading me *Treasure Island* and *Kidnapped*. My throat is very sore, but I am brought ginger ale and Jell-O, and I know I have nothing to do but lie in this beautiful bed and be read to.

Treasure Island is the book I remember best; perhaps it came first. Who, at any age, could resist those words of a menacing visitor arriving at the lonely Admiral Benbow Inn in the year of grace 17- ? Or the fearsome image the stranger provoked of a one-legged seafaring man who was to be profoundly feared, feared enough that he, in "a thousand forms," haunted the stormy nights of that cruel coast? Certainly not I, comfortably bunked in my grandmother's bed. Billy Bones, Black Dog, and Long John Silver all become real. I am on the island, startled particularly by Ben Gunn and becoming aware of what it might be to be *marooned*—the exact opposite of everything I know. I feel fear—a delicious fear which is palpable but not at all dangerous. I am, after all, in the most loving and comfortable of circumstances and I have only to receive this story from my grandmother while anchored fast in Stevenson's "pleasant land of counterpane." There is no desire or reason to be elsewhere.

I did not know then, at eight, that my grandmother was estranged from my grandfather. I did not know I even had this grandfather, who would later and without explanation appear. (My other grandfather, my father's father, had died young, long before I was born.) I never learned where this man had been or why. No one spoke of it. I knew only that first he was not there and then he was, and the adults around me acted as if that were normal. I figured out that he had come back because my grandmother could no longer take care of herself and he felt responsible. To this day, I know nothing more of his life and interests. There is no one to ask. I am alone on the rooftop.

It was not so very long after her reading *Treasure Island* to me that my grandmother lost her memory and her mind to dementia and had to be monitored constantly. She was then in a smaller apartment at 1088. My grandfather, an affable man, died taking care of her. Then my two aunts assumed the responsibility and were almost used up in the tandem process. Finally my grandmother went to a nursing home in Southampton, near Water Mill, a quiet town at the time, where she and her family had spent summers for decades. She was joined in residence by two of her sisters, but by then they did not know each other.

Another, much younger, sister developed dementia later and was kept in her New York apartment. She was the one I knew best, quick witted and exquisitely pretty, a delicate fountain of good humor: Great Aunt Emma Cuddihy Gillespie with the silky blonde hair, the one buried below my mother in the family grave at Gate of Heaven.

At the time of hearing *Treasure Island*, I did not know that my uncle Robert, who lived part of the time at my grandmother's, had had a frontal lobotomy after a mental breakdown (now known as Post Traumatic Stress Disorder) driving ambulances in the Second World War. I remember only that he took me to see National Velvet and a game at Yankee Stadium. I remember watching him construct a television, the first I had ever seen. He was tall and gentle.

I did not know that alcoholism and rapaciousness were eating away at this family, that lawsuits and acrimony were attacking it like pirates. The Cuddihy publishing fortune from

Funk & Wagnalls was washing away like gold dust after ship-wreck, and there was no one, no way to gather it back. There were only the predators. The great resiliency of my great-grandfather and his era was gone. Moreover, as was pointed out to me repeatedly and with some bitterness, federal income taxes were now a reality, and the New Deal was not a good deal for my species.

My great-grandfather had lost faith in his friend Franklin D. Roosevelt. When President Roosevelt called to invite him to the capital, R. J. Cuddihy answered, "If you want to see me, you come to my office in New York."

On the other side of my family—my father's side—re-sentments were running even stronger against Mexico, which during the revolution of 1910-1940 had appropriated without recompense the sugar plantations that were the family business. The loss of the sugar business and the ravages of the Great Depression dug deep into my family's core. My father wanted nothing more than to be a poet and a writer but went to Wall Street instead, a dutiful son, to recoup the family's finances.

Social and financial pressures were pushing my family out into new zones. Like blackbird, they needed fertile territory where they could start again and prosper. They had to move and change.

As I lay in my grandmother's bed, I knew only that I had a very sore throat but was being cared for totally; I could let go of everything but Jim Hawkins and his companions. I felt their great longing for Treasure Island but did not understand so well how they came to loathe it.

Now many years later, I have become the oldest woman in my family and the matriarch of memory. Recently I stood in the port of Everett, Washington, by the hulk of the *Equator*, the schooner that carried Robert Louis Stevenson from Hawaii through the Gilbert islands to Samoa, his final home in the South Sea islands. Later converted to a steam tug, the *Equator* was sold into the Northwest salmon trade and operated along the Alaska coast. A friend has given me a photo from the 1920's: "Tug, Equator, Entering Anchor Bay, Chignik, Alaska." Black smoke billows from the funnel, smudging into clouds, all beauty abandoned. Finally in 1958, it collapsed in Puget Sound and was scuttled outside Everett. The wrecked vessel of a great dreamer had come ashore, its cargo of untold stories long lost.

An abandoned historical preservation project, the *Equator* is visited mostly by feral cats fed by a secret caregiver. Their scattered dishes rise like small moons out of the shadows under the ship's ribs. It is said the wreck is haunted by the spirits of "Tusitala," the storyteller, and his friend, King Kalakaua of Hawaii, who came on board to say goodbye as the writer was preparing to set sail in 1889. Those entrepreneurs who chase ghosts maintain it is one of the most haunted sites in the state of Washington.

When Stevenson died at his Samoan home in 1893, he was buried on top of the mountain behind his house. The local chiefs, it is said, forbade use of firearms on the mountain from then on in order to enable the birds to sing undisturbed around his grave.

"The night fell lovely in the extreme," this restless, wandering storyteller once wrote. "After the moon went down the heaven was a thing to wonder at for stars...."

Blackbird Singing in the Dead of Night

It is the afternoon of Martin Luther King Day and two Great Egrets, four Buffleheads, and a flurry of Red-winged Blackbirds have assembled on the opposite bank. They seem to be waiting for something—a change of tide, or weather? As I watch, my thoughts wander from birds to words to politics.

"Blackbird" could be used to designate what is so common it is not seen. It also has darker connotations. "Blackbird" was an indentured servant or slave captured in the South Pacific and "Blackbirder" was another name for a slave ship or "slaver" operating in the South Pacific: Stevenson's territory.

When Paul McCartney wanted to represent the oppressed—those with broken wings—he turned to the image of blackbird. Of his song, "Blackbird," he later said:

> *I had in mind a black woman, rather than a bird. Those were the days of the civil rights movement, which all of us cared passionately about, so this was really a song from me to a black woman, experiencing these problems in the States: 'Let me encourage you to keep trying, to keep your faith, there is hope.'*
>
> (McCartney, 2001, p. 19)

McCartney first recorded his "Blackbird" song on June 11, 1968, soon after the assassination of Martin Luther King, and less than a week after the assassination of Robert F. Kennedy: so many voices stilled so suddenly.

It was four o'clock on that spring morning of June 5, 1968—not quite four hours after Robert Kennedy was shot—that my first son and second child was born. My husband Martin was taking care of our three-year-old daughter, who was admitted that same night to another hospital with croup. The medical personnel around me were absorbed with the tragedy in Los Angeles and a possible conspiracy.

I felt forgotten and alone and finally had to call out for help in order to give birth. What I remember, also, was hearing birds singing. They seemed to be filling the delivery room. It took me a long time to understand how they come to us as a greeting—a way into and out of the world—guardians of the ultimate bridge.

My son came in the time of the singing of birds, but I do not see him now, except as a memory. He chose to leave our flock and habitat. To ease the sorrow, I tell myself he left in order to establish a territory which, in some way, will strengthen our species and give us more space and opportunity. That is the way of blackbird.

If I could go back, I would ask those birds outside the hospital what I could do to help my son. Did it have something to do with the social upheaval he was born into?

Why are we born when and where we are? What mysteries do numbers hold?

Chinese lore maintains that on the eve of the seventh day of the seventh lunar month—July 7—two stars known as the Weaving Maiden and the Oxherd, lovers separated in earthly life, cross the Milky Way on a bridge made of the wings of magpies. They are allowed this one night together each year; but if it rains, the magpies are unable to make their bridge and the lovers must wait until the next year.

I know little of magpies but much of separation—the deaths and estrangements that haunt me. Would I dare a bridge of wings? The itinerant naturalists I followed—White, Lawson, and Catesby—dared oceans that were months wide, travels wide as galaxies, and risks that might have blown them into different universes. They reported and marveled. They brought back pieces of the truth stuffed in their pockets. As Enoe-Will, Lawson's assistant, put it, they "made paper speak." McCartney did, too——as well as each of us, as we make our way through greetings and departures, collecting small mementos as we go, stuffing bits and pieces in our pockets.

Look at what I pull out of mine: a photo of my father, as a boy about ten, in a sailor suit. Years later, serving in the Navy during World War II, he was stationed in Philadelphia in a military depot where there was almost nothing to do, yet no service people were allowed to read a newspaper while working. They were given figures to check that had already been thoroughly validated. I remember being told that three commanding officers in charge of this facility went mad. When the time came for splitting up family memorabilia, no one wanted this photo. Reluctantly, I took it. I could not bear to have it cast out, an orphan. There had been too much loss already. My father had abandoned my mother and moved on to another habitat. That was, sometimes, the way of blackbird.

Slow Morning

I have often heard the comment that Roger Tory Peterson made us a "world of watchers" because he provided simple guides that we all could follow. His 1934 *A Field Guide to the Birds* truly opened our eyes.

But opening your eyes is only the beginning; there is much else that goes into seeing. When you are traveling and looking for birds, you must choose your own methods to record. Do you use words or sketches or both? You must pick your subjects, concentrating on what holds most interest, then capture them as best you can, whatever your tools and protocols. Simplicity is key—and faith in yourself. Only you can make your Life List. Everything you need is right before you, but you must remember to look, record, and remain open to corrections and possibilities.

The choices you make affect your range. The more flexible you are, the greater your range. The greater your range, the more likely you are to surmount vicissitudes. The blackbird naturalist will learn how to cover a wide area of the map and to overcome thirst, drought, fever, plague, hunger, disruption, and disappointment. The blackbird observer will endure, as will blackbird.

Now, in late morning, the cordgrass is within two feet of being inundated, and already a strong wind is blowing from the Northwest—the "cold" wind of Lawson's companions. The new weather cycle is moving in quickly, sweeping the sky before it. Where does the patient Great Blue Heron go and the curious otter? Suddenly, there is nothing to look at but water, drowning grass, and sky; and here come the privateers of the north, storms sent by the jet stream to pillage the coast.

As the cold front moves in with rain, a swarm of forty cowbirds appears on the lawn, energetically feeding in the softened soil. Red-winged Blackbirds fly over them, as if monitoring, but keep their distance. The creek, at high tide, is awash, the world gray and wet. Forecasts threaten much colder temperatures and possibly snow. (How will the hummingbirds stay alive?)

If the otter spends two-thirds of its time on land, where is it now on this dark and flooded morning? It is off somewhere with the moon. It is deep in a subterranean den playing with what it has raked off the grass, a kaleidoscope of faces. It is entrancing its prisoners who do not know where they are, in a watery kingdom beyond their imagining. No shaman approaches. The captured will soon be lost forever and forgotten, their cries falling upon a silent beach.

As the day wears on, the marsh stays soaked and dark, its blood drained. A set of epaulets flashes by, and then another. I am reminded that the bank of a marsh cannot possibly be empty, even when it first appears that way, even in what we call "the dead of winter," for a marsh is very much alive. The

Red-winged Blackbirds are eating today from our neighbor's feeders. They feed with wrens and sparrows. They sing from a bare-branched tree. They tell me, listen and look: There is no dead of winter.

I Come to the Edge of America

Dawn hovers on the edge of the cold front. The lawn and the muddy banks of the river are silvered. I think there will be no birds. Then, suddenly, in front of me, with its dramatic black bands, a Killdeer. (Lawson calls it a Lap-wing or Green Plover and Catesby, the Chattering Plover.) I watch as it feeds alone in the grass. It reminds me of something.

As if they have waited for such a signal, other birds appear, cowbirds and Red-winged Blackbirds in all their color variations. There is swooping and song from the feeders out to the marsh and back. Day has broken. The birds seem to be moving with special energy, perhaps glad to be released from a cold night, perhaps sensing that colder weather is on the way. As wind begins to blow, their activity quiets and then disappears. The wind suddenly becomes a gale. Large swells move down the creek; deck furniture crashes, and snow sweeps across the scene.

Now, looking out over the marsh, I see it: the winter of 1993-94, my first winter on the South Carolina coast. Martin and I had chosen to go to Charleston and settled on Folly Beach, an island community eight miles south of the city facing the Atlantic. The residents—and the welcoming sign as you enter—call it "The Edge of America." It is a place where the uncommon Wilson's Plover winters and thoughts of the Civil War abound. (The movie *Glory* was filmed here close to the original battle site of Fort Wagner on Morris Island.) We rented a house called "Back Home" on Arctic Boulevard, all too appropriate for Alaskan visitors looking for warmth. It was a very cold winter.

The Ruddy Turnstone and Pete

One late afternoon in December, I took a walk down the beach. It was dusk, a red sun setting into gray clouds and water. Suddenly, as I approached the curving end of the island, I came across a colony of Ruddy Turnstones with their bright colors and calico patterns. I watched in fascination as they darted about their business, searching the rocky, muddy beach for food. They paid no attention to me: I was, as they would say in Charleston, "from off." I watched for a long time, trying to remember their field marks and behavior so that I could validate my identification.

Catesby made a special note of the behavior of Ruddy Turnstones (which he called the Turn-stone, or Sea-dottrel). In 1722, on a trip off the coast of Florida, he observed a Ruddy Turnstone which landed on his ship and was captured:

> *It was very active in turning up stones, which we put into its cage; but not finding under them the usual food, it died. In this action it moved only the upper mandible; yet would with great dexterity and quickness turn over stones of above three pounds weight. This property Nature seems to have*

given it for finding of its food, which is probably worms and
insects on the seashore.

(Catesby, p. 44)

What Catesby didn't say—because he didn't know—is that this amazing bird can open barnacles, dig holes larger than itself, and fly at 40 mph.

As astronomer-philosopher Chet Raymo points out, our ignorance grows as our knowledge grows; and that is a good thing. Ignorance, he says, is "a vessel waiting to be filled, permission for growth, a ground for the electrifying encounter with mystery."

I thought of Pete Isleib, my recently deceased birding acquaintance, and how he was in another settlement, a fully engaged village like that of the birds but one I could not see. Somewhere, on the other side of mystery, he was walking around observing, identifying by shape, size, and behavior species we cannot know or name.

I turned around and saw the moon, rising in the east. I walked home in the moon's light thinking of Pete and where he was and all that is winged and invisible in that world out of our reach. I wanted him to know I had binoculars now and tried to keep them with me. I was beginning to watch birds. I was beginning to *look*, and I think he would have been pleased. We were out of the office now; we were in the field together. I was walking home with the moon to a rented house on the Edge of America. I was building a Life List.

Setting Out

Now, as I look out over the marsh, it is March 18, 1993, the winter before we went to Folly Beach. Riding the wake of an epic blizzard dubbed a "white hurricane," I have just arrived in New York to visit my mother after a winter in the West Indies. I had been in Antigua and also Nassau and had sailed in the same waters where Catesby had observed the migrating "rice-birds" and set forth his theory of "birds of passage." I had spent weeks in Tortola visiting the botanical gardens and marveling at the butterflies. I found a feral cat there and named her Blossom. She bit me.

Leaving the sailboat behind, I was full of the scents and sights of the pirate-ridden, slave-tainted, brilliantly painted Caribbean and wanted to know more. I wanted to relive those images in the midst of Manhattan in winter. There was one way:

I take my mother with me to the American Museum of Natural History to inspect their volumes (1705 and 1719) of Merian's *Metamorphosis Insectorum Surinamensium*—the books that awakened Nabokov and the books I longed to see and touch.

I can barely keep from exclaiming as I turn the ancient pages and experience the eruption of color: pineapple, passion fruit, banana, orange, grape, potato, cassava, and everywhere lizards, moths, butterflies, cockroaches, flies, spiders, and beetles, all bursting out of the volumes and escaping past my dazed eyes. I am experiencing, perhaps, some of what Nabokov experienced as an eight-year-old child in his country house outside St. Petersburg when he found the startling books.

I do not know what my mother thinks, but I am glad I have brought her. She was always comfortably at home in the museums and institutions of the city. Later, riding the bus back to her place in the bitterly cold weather, I watch a woman trying to protect a bouquet of red tulips on her lap. I think of how tulips are said to have come from the Pamir Alai Mountain Range between Turkey and Russia and can well survive a blanket of snow; I recall the myth that these flowers sprung from drops of love-crossed blood. I think of Merian's fascination with tulips and where it led her. She divorced her husband—extraordinary for her day—and traveled where her passion dictated—the wilds of a distant jungle. My mother and I boarded a city bus—such small steps.

There are tulips—white tulips—on the coffee table at my mother's apartment in front of the couch where I sleep. I have bought them for her because they are her favorite flower. I wake up next to them, trying to remember a dream that has to do with swans: perhaps a scene from a childhood visit to my grandmother's house in Water Mill when my Aunt Aime, my mother's sister, was caring for a cygnet wounded by a snapping turtle. I remember being warned of the strength of a swan's wings, being told they could break your arm. I remember the crabs we pursued with nets from a rowboat and how they turned red when we dropped them, legs struggling, into a large pot of boiling water. I remember the flow from the brackish lake out towards the Atlantic Ocean. The white tulips are stretching out of their vase in every direction, their long necks growing wild and weak. They want to tell me something. Remember, they say, remember.

I remember that rowboat, wooden and white; seaweed that came up on the oars; shadowy turtles under the surface; how water dripped from the oars when we raised them; and the sound of the oarlocks turning. The more I concentrate on this memory, the more real it becomes until I can almost smell and feel the strings of seaweed we pull up. The people come up to me, too: my young mother with such unknown paths ahead of her; her two sisters who both married late in life and had no children. These memories begin to hurt. I push them aside and try to focus on what is in front of me—hot house tulips with dangerously weak necks. I prefer the "broken" tulips, sliced with different colors that were so popular in 17th century Holland. But ass much as I like them, I am glad Merian did not get trapped by tulips and the mania for them that swept across Europe. She might have painted them over and over and never gone beyond, never stopping to watch with wonder what was crawling up their stems and down their leaves and preparing to change utterly. Undoubtedly, she would not have died in poverty, but how much less her life would have been, stripped of that mystery.

Her three early flower books (1675, 1677, and 1680) to-gether are known as *Neues Blumen Buch* or, *The New Flower Book*. In 1679 came her first book on caterpillars: Raupen, or *The Wonderful Transformation of Caterpillars and [Their] Singular Plant Nourishment*. Here, she began to waken Catesby, shake Linnae-us, and set fire to the heart of the Czar.

Two weeks pass, while I continue visiting relatives and friends and libraries and museums. Merian's work, so coveted by the royal families of Russia and England, is hard to find in the United States, and I was growing frustrated and discouraged over not being able to secure an English translation of the journal found in St. Petersburg.

On April 5th, I realized my mother's memory was failing. At lunch that day with friends at the Metropolitan Museum she had difficulty answering certain simple questions our friends asked, such as, what schools her three children had attended. I knew right away what had happened; a prickling sensation gathered at the back of my head.

Later, as we walked home through Central Park, we con-tinued to talk as if nothing had changed. It was a lovely clear day. We stopped and sat on a bench—one that happened to be inscribed, "In loving memory of Priscilla G., 1970-91, from A.G.M. who adored her." Sitting there, we looked at the trees in bud, the snowdrops and crocuses in bloom, and the spar-rows and pigeons swooping for crumbs.

This was no time to say goodbye—there was no dock from which to wave—but I knew already she had left, a small ship of discovery pulling out into the harbor, sealed orders not yet opened. I wondered what was going to happen, now that she had started her final expedition, the one she had feared for so long. Unlike Merian's, it was an expedition she would have done anything to avoid; there was no one to accompany her, nothing to bring back, and everything to lose.

Perhaps somewhere here is an image to save: my mother just before her memory crumbled, sitting on a park bench in spring; a woman cradling red tulips on her lap while riding a city bus through snowy streets; white tulips trying to escape from a vase; the shocking color of Merian's Surinam jungle creatures blazing from the thick pages; reading, in an exhibit at the New York Public Library, that texts by Thomas Mann were smuggled into Nazi Germany in 1939 in packets of tomato seeds.

I might have taken my mother birding. Central Park, with its 843 acres in the middle of the city, is one of the best places in the country to watch for birds—and not just for the historic famous pair of Red-tailed Hawks, Pale Male and Lola, that lived on the edge of a Fifth Avenue apartment building with their offspring. The park hosts over 200 species. It was April. We might have observed a Wood Thrush (now seriously in decline) or Eastern Phoebe, perhaps a Baltimore Oriole— most colorful of the blackbirds—offering us an inexplicable gift of song. Perhaps a feather might have touched her cheek and saved her, but it didn't.

The Angel of Forgetfulness

In Jewish lore there is the story of the Angel of Forgetfulness who kisses a soul on the lips before the soul returns from heaven to earth.

I think this angel, blown off course by storms of emotion, had mistakenly entered an Irish Catholic home. I think she kissed my mother on the lips that spring. It might have been while my mother slept, or while she sat on a park bench observing the joggers, the dogs, the bicyclists, the skateboarders, and the strollers moving by in their endless progression; or maybe it happened while she bowed her head in prayer at her church, St. Thomas More. It might have been in the late winter blizzard just before I arrived to visit; or maybe while I was turning over the pages of Merian's *Metamorphosis* as she sat beside me. There is no telling when a vagrant will arrive from a foreign shore or what its behavior will be.

Clearly, whenever it happened, the angel felt content and stayed, leading my mother back into the past and beyond, feeding on her memories, sucking away at her story.

Some say the angel slaps the baby at birth, either on the mouth or the nose, causing it to forget the Torah, which it has learned while in the womb. Learning then becomes a recollection.

Some say the name of the Angel of Forgetfulness is Poteh or Purah. Some say it is a demon, not an angel. Myriad incantatory lists, elaborate classifications, and explanations of angels exist. There is an angel *of* or *over* everything—anger, storms, lost objects—similar to the roster of saints I was brought up with in childhood. But no Linnaeus of the higher life forms exists, no taxonomy to take us past the Seraphim and the Cherubim into the indistinct species. The study of angels is perched at the level where Catesby's study of Bobolinks reached in 1725: We know, when they fly away for the winter, they are not hiding in caves, hollow trees, or under water, but we cannot understand their patterns of flight because of "the immenseness of the globe" and "the vast tracts of land remaining unknown but to its barbarous natives."

Synchronicity

Serendipitously, the American Museum of Natural History put out a calendar for the year following my museum visit with twelve plates from Merian's *Metamorphosis*. I began, that January, charting my days amid her twisting leaves and feeding caterpillars. Under the wild tendrils of the *Marquiaas*, "preferable to the passion flower," this list: *Call Nora, Pat, Melody, Tom. Pick up suit.* I returned, that month, from my stay on Folly Beach—my first winter visit to the Carolina coast—and was once more in New York.

Janus, looking forwards and backwards, is the two-faced Roman god of gates and doors, guardian of exits and entrances. And January, it seems, is often a time of setting out.

John Lawson departed Charleston on December 28, 1700, on his epic journey into the Carolina backcountry. It was January 1712 when "Tuscarora Jack" Barnwell forced his way inland in pursuit of Lawson's murderers. Catesby made sure he visited areas of interest in different seasons in order to get as complete a view as possible. From the Bahamas he brought back important news of winter migration. And it was January when Merian died, her bright, tropical work migrating to the coldest of countries.

Now I had taken to winter trips across the country—from my home in Alaska and later my home in the Northwest—to the East Coast. I nearly always started in January, and year after year these trips began to add up in my notebooks: the birds seen, the places visited, conversations overheard, bits and pieces beginning to form maps of range and migration: an atlas of memory in the making.

The Angel Grows More Insistent

It was May 1999 when my mother collapsed, mentally and physically, and I went to assist her. She had been prescribed 75 milligrams daily of Amitriptyline, an anti-depressant and a disaster. When she started to come back from this debilitating treatment, she was composed, relatively lucid, and beginning to walk with a cane. The long line of nurses had begun, first by day and then by day and night. They came from an agency which employed Irish nurse-companions, not registered nurses. My mother fought the necessity of a night nurse. Long, angry phone calls ensued as we attempted to convince her of their need. There were also nurses whom we did not want.

In June, I visited again. We walked and sat on inscribed park benches: *Elizabeth & Patrick, October 15, 1985; That my grandchildren might love Central Park; "I loaf and invite my soul."* More than 1,200 benches out of the 9,000 in the park had been "adopted" and inscribed at that point. I had sat on many of these with my mother and walked by hundreds more. I wrote down what they said and wondered who had sat on them before and wondered what images lingered, what crowds of desire and longing followed us home, crying out to be comforted. Was there a beautiful land they had moved to, or was it simply "poo-jok," or mist?

Back in the Northwest, summer found its way. I tried to concentrate on gardening. We had moved from Alaska to the state of Washington, and here was my first opportunity, as I saw it, to establish a garden. I remember standing out in the flower beds at night with our Weimaraner puppy, Gus, listening to the bell buoy out in the bay ringing and a freight train passing. I might be standing next to the Tall Bearded Iris or the tightly budded delphinium or the peripatetic foxglove. Sometimes all was quiet and heavy with moisture. I would think about what my neighbor had told me of his experiences with spirit beings and the mother raccoon who comes at night to wash her three babies in his bird bath.

I wondered at the crowdedness of the garden, how we could all fit there together pursuing our many different activities on separate levels and not bump into each other. From time to time, the bell buoy would ring or, down along the shore, a freight train would pass. Yes, the night was crowded, and my heart. The night fell lovely all around me, a starry shower of memories.

I would call my mother. Often she sounded tired and never wanted to talk for long. She remembered the old days when long distance calls were expensive. I would visit when I could. I talked with doctors, by phone and in person. There were many, many tests and few results.

The summer stumbled by. The tall apartment buildings of the foxgloves opened and closed their units from the bottom of the stalk up to the very top. Bees and hummingbirds visited their damask innards and, more rarely, butterflies.

It was the summer John F. Kennedy, Jr., his wife and sister-in-law died in a plane crash off Martha's Vineyard and their funeral was held at my mother's church, St. Thomas More, where later she would lie. And it was the thirtieth anniversary of the Apollo 11 astronauts landing on the Sea of Tranquility.

Every day is the anniversary of something. It is a question of where to focus and what to write in the date book—what you wish to carry with you out of the jungle and record in your field notes. Every year is Stevenson's year of grace—that once-upon-a-time flow that carries you from the stormy night on the Bristol road to forever.

In August I am back in New York and again early in September.

At home, the garden bows to hydrangea, nasturtium, and sedum, the late-blooming flowers for which I am always especially grateful.

One day late in September, I awake to a world of fog and sparkling spider webs, some the size of dinner plates, riding high in the huge Douglas firs. It is time, I know, for the hungry spiders to eat meat enough to get them through the winter. All this beauty is simply biological necessity. Insects are being devoured so that spiders may weave and satisfy their appetite. Death is feeding on a morning of dewy lace, and the neighbors are exclaiming. Maria Sybilla Merian would have gotten out her art supplies and gone immediately to work.

The neurologist calls. He assumes my mother has a mild form of Alzheimer's. He prescribes Aricept. Now the dance of drugs begins as the filaments of my mother's mind unravel more swiftly. More Amitriptyline. Ziprexa. Aricept. A mixed flock of brightly colored pills organized by feeding cycle: these once a day; those three times; this with that; that with this.

October arrives. Dahlias continue to bloom, some large as saucers. Conditions with my mother worsen. My daughter gives birth to a son. Our flock is continually expanding and shrinking in size, buffeted by events but always moving.

Conversations with my mother tend to be confused, tangled, and circular, while once they had been placid and purposeful, with ripples of humor. The Angel of Forgetfulness stands larger over her, growing as my mother's memory shrinks, absorbing her. Soon there will be nothing left but the pieces I remember from what she told me, like feathers scattered on the ground. And then the Angel will come looking for me, and I will have forgotten its silhouette, its flight pattern, its call. I have neglected to make proper notes. Invisible and silent, it may sneak up on me at any time and grab me with its fatal talons.

Late in November I plant tulip bulbs. I continue planting them into December.

I read a story in *Green Prints* magazine of a woman who was planting tulip bulbs at 5:00 p.m. on December 19 in Minnesota. The soil has not yet frozen and she has just received a divorce. There is a pink glow in the western sky, she writes.

I look at the gardening catalogs over and over with all their pictures of tulips: Which will I choose to bloom in my

garden? If I could choose only one, which one would it be—
Apeldoorn Elite, Single Late Dreamland, Astarte? I put the
catalogs away while thinking of Maria Sybilla Merian and how
she persisted, even when in the grips of malaria.

The year turns and the millennium. I travel to South Carolina, visiting my mother from there, learning the schedules of
Amtrak, the night voyages through dark swamps and small
towns, the same country penetrated by Lawson and Catesby.
Here, I listen for whispering wings and the distant cry of the
Ivory-billed Woodpecker, whose beak, Catesby tells us, was
much sought after by the *Canada Indians*

> *... who make Coronets of 'em for their great princes and
> great warriors, by fixing them round a Wreath, with their
> points outward. The Northern Indians, having none of
> these Birds in their cold country, purchase them of the
> Southern People at the price of two, and sometimes three
> Buck-skins a Bill.*
>
> (Catesby, p. 88)

Some reputable ornithologists still believe that the "Ghost
Bird of the Southern Swamps" is not extinct but manages to
survive in tangled, flooded hardwood areas of the Southeast.
Some seek it now in the rugged mountains of eastern Cuba,
where verified sightings were made in 1986. Here is the Virginia Dare of the bird world. Just enough clues, just enough
video footage, just enough uncertain photos, just enough hope
exists to keep the search going.

Back home in the Northwest, I return to the garden. With my mother, there are calls and occasional visits, sometimes happy, sometimes not. There are conversations sometimes of rage and confusion and paranoia and resentment; mostly, they are pleasant and superficial, looping in ever smaller circles, the same questions asked and answered over and over. The medications pile up; at one point, there are seventeen. The final one will be morphine.

The Angel of Forgetfulness has grown ever more insistent, pushing my mother out of the nest, a giant cowbird making ever greater demands. Still, I cannot identify it or determine its migratory path. I cannot tell which nest it will rob next but fear it is my own.

My Mother Dies

Yes, the time for morphine came—the liquid form known as Roxinal, placed by dropper under the tongue. Caregivers of the elderly are entirely familiar with it, but our two caregivers, not registered nurses, refused to handle it. My sister, taking responsibility and following the instructions of Hospice, began to administer it herself. I quickly made arrangements to return to New York and took dual charge of the small brown bottle.

I knew my mother would want to see a priest, and we went to considerable effort to find one who could visit her in time. Talk with her, we asked, and pray, but do not tell her you are giving her the last rites. That would frighten her.

My mother died on Sunday, August 4, 2002, late in the morning, after the priest had left and as I talked with her and held her. She coughed and gasped as her congested heart gave out. It was not what I would describe as an easy death. She called out to my father, who had abandoned her, and to the secondary nurse who was there but who had spent less time with her than the principal nurse who was absent. My son Sam was with us. My sister had gone to run an errand, along with my daughter. The nurse on duty did not believe her patient had died, but she had. Sam and I carried her limp and surprisingly heavy body from the living room, where we had all been sitting, to the bedroom. There was no sound or sense that anything was different.

I acted on the instructions from Hospice. I poured the remaining morphine down the drain and called the funeral home, Frank E. Campbell, just down the street. Their representatives came and removed her body; I followed soon after to go choose a coffin.

My mother would have laughed. As I hurried down the crowded sidewalk along Madison Avenue, I almost ran into Woody Allen, walking towards me with his wife and daughter: a Manhattan moment.

But she would not have laughed at what happened next. Her principal caregiver—I shall call her Patricia—accused me of hastening my mother's death with morphine. Patricia, who had been with my mother for more than three years, was not with her when she died; the weekend nurse was on duty.

Even before this weekend, Patricia could not accept that my mother was dying and kept complaining that the doctors were not doing enough. My mother's "sudden death," according to her, was my fault. She wrote to me and other members of my family and threatened to go beyond.

I knew she had truly loved my mother and that this was a form of grieving. I also knew she could not go far because she was not a registered but a practical nurse and had limited medical training, knowledge, and qualifications. On our side, as her employer, we had carefully followed all the requirements for

taxes and Social Security. We gave her and the relief nurse generous bequests with our sincere gratitude—my mother would
have wanted that. There was no reason to feel guilty or to feel
regret for our actions. Still, she had stung us badly at a time
when we were most vulnerable.

Stories of morphine misuse pop up in the news. Soon after
I arrived back in South Carolina, one appeared in the Charleston paper of a nurse arrested for stealing morphine from her
patients in a hospital. Another, more infamous one, involved
a British nurse, Sister Kathleen Atkinson, charged with with-
drawing morphine from a number of patients in order to give
one patient a fatal overdose. Murder charges were dropped
for lack of evidence, but Atkinson lost her license. After Hurricane Katrina, a New Orleans doctor and two nurses were
charged with murdering four stranded patients by administer-
ing lethal doses of morphine mixed with a sedative. Now the
Right-to-Die movement blurs the lines between murder and
death with dignity and between suicide and crime. I leave it to
others to argue the points.

From the Carolina marsh, I had long telephone conversations with my family in New York about Patricia and what
needed to be done: Could she make trouble, or was she simply
flailing in a hurtful but ineffective way? Should I ignore her
and her charges or did I need to confront her?

It was time to do something: I would write her a letter.
First, we decided, we needed to acknowledge her pain and
thank her for her continuing loyalty to my mother, her prayers
and offerings of Mass. Then, we must set the record straight:

how we worked with my mother's doctors and with Hospice; what we all did, specifically, to alleviate the unbearable pain our mother experienced in her last days as her heart and lungs gave out; why we chose not to send her to the hospital but to keep her, as she wished, at home. Finally, we must assure Patricia that my mother's death was not her fault but a natural process in which we all share; and that it is difficult to live so close to the end of a life as Patricia did day by day with a rapidly failing patient.

I carefully wrote the letter—by hand—carefully addressed it and stamped it and sent it on its way to Patricia in Ireland. I knew I would never hear back and I never did.

What was I chasing, a *Fata Morgana* of reconciliation? Did I see a distant land of forgiveness and compassion that did not exist? Was mine a journey of delusion?

Blackbird: Migration and Its Hazards

Birds migrate between breeding and wintering areas in extraordinary numbers. Sibley, echoing Catesby, says, "The number of birds taking part in this semi-annual event is so enormous, and the geographic territory they cover so vast, that it is difficult to gain a clear perspective on the process from any one vantage point." (*The Sibley Guide to Bird Life and Behavior*, p. 59) Many do not return; perhaps as many as half the songbirds that travel from the Northern Hemisphere are lost each spring.

Most travel at night, when there is less turbulence, but some travel nonstop. Some, like the Red-winged Blackbird and the Bobolink, are driven by time concerns, needing to get to their breeding grounds ahead of the females.

Ornithologists who watch the skies from oil platforms in the Gulf of Mexico tell what happens when storms, strong head winds, or sudden cold temperatures weaken birds as they flap their way across the 600 mile ocean path: Many fall as a rain of colorful and varied species——lower and lower—until they hit the deck of the rig. Certain hummingbirds, such as the Red-throated, make this tortuous trip. It seems impossible. Along the mountainous coast of Southeast Alaska a long-held folk theory explains: Hummingbirds fly north each spring on the backs of the Sandhill Cranes.

Destruction of tropical rain forest and subtropical habitat can rob south-bound birds of nutrition and strength just as development of their northern nesting areas can deny them the opportunity to breed and survive.

Endless hazards intrude, from communications towers to wind turbines. Cities, with their multiple dangers, represent special challenges, including high-rise buildings and their lights. Volunteers for the Chicago Bird Collision Monitors, a group working with Chicago Audubon, fan through the city during spring and fall mornings to find victims. One volunteer reports collecting 600 injured and 700 dead birds during one spring migration. (*Audubon*, Nov.-Dec. 2008, p. 84)

"Green" buildings, calling for more glass, only increase the problem. Daniel Klem, Jr., of Muhlenberg College, estimates that every year at least a billion birds die by colliding with windows, a manmade cause of death second only to habitat loss. (*Audubon*, Nov.-Dec. 2008, p. 85) Countless others are injured.

While neither glass technology nor green building codes have responded adequately to the need, sometimes the answer is as simple as pulling down the blinds or turning off the lights. Chicago, Toronto, New York, Detroit, Cleveland, and San Francisco are among cities working on a "lights-out" plan.

My Travel Plans Change

It was the last day of January 2003, not quite six months since my mother had died, and I had returned to my Pacific Northwest home on the Washington coast. For the first time in ten years of winter traveling, I had not gone to New York. My needs had changed.

I was beginning to move my boundaries and seek new habitat—to stretch. I was learning an all-important lesson of blackbird: You need to keep moving forward even if you do not know the name or the nature of the place you are headed towards; and you need to travel as light as you can. The lighter your burden, the greater your range.

As I walked around the house greeting the animals and touching what I found important, I tried to remember my different trips back and forth across the country—what happened each year, how they were different, one from another. Maybe I could not remember like Nabokov ("the gruel-like mess of broken brown blossoms under the lilacs") but I could, if I tried, put the years in order and establish a chronology. This was not to say that I considered time of paramount importance: No. But chronology was a method I used to record what I saw flitting over the marsh. There might be no such thing as past nor future beyond human consciousness but still, I would continue to build my list.

Blackbird: As Dark Energy

In spite of living in an age of complex information, I can see only so far and understand only so much. The universe, it is said, is like an expanding balloon or soap bubble, each dot on its skin moving further away from every other dot, and each star from each star. If only we could discover the nature of the dark energy which propels the universe or the mysterious dark matter that fills it, perhaps we could know our fate. How and why is the universe expanding so rapidly? I don't know, and still I must push on, an expedition of one towards an unknown land, or a land that perhaps does not exist——another *Fata Morgana*.

How do we begin to describe what we do not know or what might not exist? What words do we use? If I have no adequate words, how can I think about or explore the subject? Where is my notebook, like the one John Lawson carried, carefully setting down in columns the words of three tribes he dealt with—"Tuskeruro" (Tuscarora); "Pampticough" (Pamlico); "Woccon"?

One	*unche*	*weembot*	*tonne*
Fire	*utchar*	*tinda*	*yau*
Water	*awoo*	*umpe*	*ejau*

Where do I set the sound-words of the birds? Lawson himself stated that "their musical notes & cryes must not be omitted," and Sibley will tell you how important it is to learn to identify birds by their sounds. When you start out, it seems impossible.

Of the Northern Mockingbird, Catesby said the name the Indians gave it was *"cencontlatolly,* or four hundred tongues," the approximate number, it turns out, of bird species in the area at that time.

Does the Red-winged Blackbird truly speak in three syllables? How do we spell these syllables? Is it "o-ka-lee" or "kon-ka-ree"? And how does the song of the female differ from that of the male? Does the male Bobolink really whistle "seeyew" and sing "bob-o-link-link-Lincoln"? The answer can carry great weight, for sometimes vocalization will determine species; and the naming of birds is not quite fixed, any more than measurement of the intelligence of birds is fixed. We are humbled by recent discoveries. Once you see a song in print, that is how you tend to hear it; you are deafened by language you have and blinded by language you don't have.

Just as there is new interest in studying the brains of birds, there is new interest in analyzing the songs of birds. One commentator, philosopher and musician David Rothenberg, asserts, "Bird song is something you must reach out to love before it will reveal itself to you." (*Why Birds Sing,* p. 42) Here are mysteries whose thresholds of awe we can only approach, mysteries for which we have no words. In laboratories across the country, the brains and songs of birds are being dissected, while almost everywhere—from porches and to fields—we are listening. Meanwhile, the two "Voyager" spacecraft launched in 1977 continue to carry recordings of bird song and animal noises as well as messages in 55 languages into the furthest reaches of space.

Since invention of the tape recorder, many birders have captured the sounds of birds, and some have had unexpected experiences while doing so. In 1959, Friedrich Jurgenson, a Swedish film producer, was recording bird songs when he discovered he had picked up disembodied voices as well. Experimenting with radio wavelengths, he expanded his collection. He claimed he had found the voice of his mother who had been dead for four years: "Friedrich, you are being watched. Friedel, my little Friedel, can you hear me?" Yes, Friedrich heard her, he said, and the era of Electronic Voice Phenomena and Instrumental Transcommunication was born.

Voices from another dimension were crowding in on electromagnetic waves, it was said, and finding outlet through tape recorders, computers, faxes, and televisions. There were advocates who were convinced that Thomas Edison had worked on, or at least conceived of, a "telephone to the dead," though no plans have been found. Others, convinced that conversation with "the dead" was possible, invented their own devices. Bird song and spirit word, it began to appear, inhabited the same space—and that space was our space, the field of everything.

Perhaps birds and their songs are closer to the heart of reality than anything else. String theory proponents tell us there is only one substance, called strings, which vibrate and make the universe a symphony: This cosmic music, then, must be the mind of God. Who is to say the mind of God is not expressed through the throat of birds? Or that birds are not the true link between heaven and earth? Didn't Aristophanes tell us that birds, born of Chaos and Eros, were first to see the light? Rothenberg states, "If the works of God are to be heard on Earth, there is no better place to find them than in the deep intricacies of incomprehensible bird song." (p. 218)

Just as it is hard to describe what you think you hear or to define the wordless, it is also hard to capture what you think you see. Each observer will bring different strengths and weaknesses to the exercise, resulting in different outcomes.

John White was adept at quick field sketches later transformed into watercolors at a time when watercolors were not commonly used. He was also a talented map maker able to transfer topography to paper quickly. *Speed* was his greatest asset.

My guides searched at a time when little was clear, nothing was easy, and their professional world was caught up in a profound argument: What was most important, to name the creature correctly or to depict it in its natural setting? Petiver, the influential London collector, wanted to reorganize Merian's work, but organization was not her concern. Her concern was the miracle of metamorphosis. She sought the "wonderful transformation."

Catesby wanted not *landscape* but *birdscape*, the dynamism of the universe of birds. He wanted to show the bird in its natural setting, demonstrating its connection with habitat.

Comprehension was his strength. And Lawson? I would have to say *energy* and *dedication* were his attributes.

I struggle with all of this. My method is journals, notes, and calendars, small paper frames I place around personal events, usually done hurriedly and often tenuously. I cannot find words for what lies beyond me—the energy patterns dancing across the marshes—nor can I name their nature any more than scientists today can name dark matter. But I can describe what I see and put that in the context of what I know, my own cabinet of curios. I can study these patterns and see where they begin to lead. I can consider relationships as a kind of map. I can start out again and again on expedition, setting forth through the gate of memory.

Riding the Famine Roads

I was learning to go backwards as well as forwards, even if doing so added miles to my trip and exposed me to additional dangers. I remembered how Lawson, struggling through the swollen Carolina rivers, thought he had traveled twice as far as he actually had and how White, "Governor of the Lost," kept trying to circle back to his colony.

I needed to go to Ireland, not so much for genealogy and history as for atmosphere. I wanted to breathe some Irish air and connect with my blackbird cousins.

Six faithful family members joined me for a horseback riding tour of the western coast. Not all were accomplished equestrians, but we made the trip safely. Hour by hour we rode along narrow roads and over spongy trails that gave way to rocky trails through the inhospitable area known as the Burren. We passed some of the three thousand sacred wells in the country. We passed collapsing stone churches, and one foggy day we traveled along a series of the "Famine Roads."

These strange roads and walls, found throughout the southwest of Ireland, are cruel reminders of the Great Hunger. Narrow passages with stone fences on either side, they lead, for the most part, nowhere but to twisting dead-ends up on the steep hillsides. These are the result of the prevailing political and social sentiment that a person had to work in order to receive government assistance and, since there was no real work, they were ordered to build roads in exchange for food. These roads, serving little purpose but forced labor, were the ultimate journey of delusion, a gigantic stone *Fata Morgana*.

The slick ground was rocky and difficult to manage, even for the steady and sure-footed Irish horses. The view, too, was rocky and difficult——moldering stone fences on either side of the narrow roads and, scattered over the empty hills, the roofless and tumbledown cottages. Our guide told us that up to a dozen people would live in such a dwelling. If they were fortunate enough to own one, their Connemara pony would join them inside "for warmth and comfort."

I had had a pony as a girl——a show pony named Little Breeches, whose coat gleamed when we groomed her. She won ribbon after ribbon, and sometimes silver-plated cups. But I had never been hungry and feared for my survival—not like this. I wanted to thank my blackbird family. Somehow they had escaped the famine and disease, the workhouses and soup kitchens, crossed an ocean, established a new life in New York, acquired a high level of education, achieved and lost a fortune, and given me the chance to continue their travels. I could see now that it was my responsibility, not just my curiosity, that propelled me to make my journey. My model could well be Lawson, who sailed to America almost on a whim but who then gave his life to studying and reporting on its wonders.

Before we left Ireland, we stopped in the town of Kilkenny. My brother, who researched the matter, had told me that Kilkenny was the ancestral home of the Cuddihy family, but no clues remained as to where they had gone or when. With the crumbling of churches and their records, there was little evidence that they had ever existed.

I remembered I was told, as a child, that at Ellis Island the Cuddihys were separated into two groups——my people with our spelling and the others listed as "Cudahy." I was told the other family continued west and became the wealthy Chicago meat-packing family. Imagine a clerk at Ellis Island having such divine power. Imagine being defined by a twist of spelling—one that would determine whether you would be a publisher or a butcher. But blackbird is like that——buffeted by wind and chance but always moving forward.

We ambled about the town of Kilkenny with no specific plan. Then we saw them——a number of brass nameplates on front doors announcing "Cuddihy." I stood in front of one for some time and wondered what would happen if I knocked on the door and introduced myself with the greeting, "I'm here! I'm home!"

I will never know, because I did not try it, but that is part of the magic of blackbird: The choices are endless and their shape is constantly changing. In memory I can go back and knock on one of those doors at any time.

I cannot say it is wrong to go one way instead of another. I think of those itinerant naturalists. They would not have considered themselves lost just because they were exploring in a place where no one else had been before. *Do not be afraid*, they tell me. Or as poet David Wagoner states, "The forest knows/ where you are. You must let it find you."

I Meet Maggie Fox

When my family and I returned to New York, we immediately changed planes for Buffalo. We were headed to Lily Dale, home of the Spiritualists. Spiritualists believe there is no "death" and that it is possible to communicate with the "dead." For some time I had wanted to find out more about them.

I was especially interested in an unlikely figure—Maggie Fox (1833—1893), considered the founder of Spiritualism in the United States and lover of celebrated explorer Elisha Kent Kane.

Maggie led a short life of fame, notoriety, alcoholism, and poverty, but she stirred the nation and held my attention. I felt I had to meet her as part of my own journey, no matter where it led.

The home of Spiritualism is the hamlet of Lily Dale in southwestern New York. Its winter counterpart is Cassadaga, an even smaller village located in central Florida. We were among the more than 20,000 visitors who make a trip to Lily Dale each summer, and we were to make a number of trips to Cassadaga.

What did I see when we arrived? A quiet, weathered Victorian village looking as if it were not in any hurry, and dirt paths bordered by vigorous day lilies. The paths took us to the houses of the psychics, mediums, and healers who live and work there. (No one can work at Lily Dale unless certified by a board of practitioners.)

We began to knock on the doors of these houses to make appointments. Within a few hours we had all experienced the essence of Lily Dale: communications with the "Dead." I had been leery of the process but soon grew comfortable with it. You knock, or telephone, make an appointment, and when the time comes, enter the house of the specialist you have chosen. (You can do a session by telephone as well.) You settle on the time you wish and the payment, always a moderate amount. It is obvious that the residents of Lily Dale are not getting rich.

I had chosen John White, a well-known medium, who greeted me graciously as he led me into his pleasantly crowded office. I could not but help being drawn by his name, the same as the "Governor of the Lost." I told him what I wanted: to meet Maggie Fox. I could not ask for my mother. I am not sure why, but I felt I could not risk it. To stay academic would be safer, and I had been researching Maggie Fox for years. I should be able to tell right away if White's connection was real.

It took a while. Other spirits came forward, and John conveyed their greetings. Apparently they laughed when Maggie finally responded. "She's always late," they said, a fact that was corroborated by my earlier research. But now she was present, apparently, because John could see and hear her. He served as the bridge between us, posing our questions and relaying her answers.

Finally, after many inquiries, I had him ask what I had been trying to discover for years: Did she marry Elisha Kent Kane as she had always maintained? "No," she answered, "but I spent time with him." I asked about a child. John said he sensed a child with her. When I asked, Maggie said the child had been raised by others. These simple answers fully satisfied my intuition. I had been poring through books and letters, newspapers and genealogies for years pursuing these unknowns, trying to set the record straight for Maggie Fox. I had traveled to libraries across the country to delve into their deepest reservoirs of history. Now I had learned that all I had to do was ask the subject. It was like birdwatching: You need to focus on the subject and have your questions answered directly. Pictures and papers do only so much. And may distract from your efforts and confuse identification.

At the table-tipping séance we attended later, I once more asked for Maggie instead of my mother or my brother. Again, I felt conflicted. Louis Gates, the medium leading the séance, instructed the twenty or so of us in the small, darkened room to stand around the heavy oak table in the center. We were to take turns asking direct questions to a specific spirit. The table would answer "Yes" by moving or "No" by staying still.

Again, I connected with Maggie. At times the table careened wildly, pushing us up against the walls. The most frequently asked question was, "Were you murdered?" The answer invariably was a powerful movement by the table. There was crying and gasping. I thought of my brother; I was sure he had been murdered, but I could not ask.

From that room, tributaries led into dark swampy areas or perhaps frozen seas. To proceed, I would need not only guides but guardians. I would need something more than a canoe and a rifle.

Lost in the Woods

In January of 1701, John Lawson and his crew, along with his spaniel bitch, were pushing by canoe away from the shore into unknown spaces in interior Carolina. There was no way to tell what lay ahead, what hostile tribes might leap out of the tangle at any moment.

The professional surveyor and naturalist did not record his emotions; but he must have sat erect with every sense heightened, his eyes on the dog as well as on the expanse of cordgrass, watching for birds in sudden, frightened flight, the signal of danger. For Lawson, there was to be a productive period of ten more years of writing, publishing, and surveying; a period, too, of love, union, and children, not to mention the amassing of enough property to require the writing of a will.

There is no record for other matters, or a name for the spaniel bitch, to complement the abundant news of a fabulous new-found land, home to the "long black Snake" which will "coil himself under the Hen, in the Nest, where sometimes the Housewife finds him." There also were the Rattle Snakes, which have "the Power, or Art...to charm Squirrels, Hares, Partridges, or any such thing, in such a manner, that they run directly into their Mouths." And there was the "Al-legator" too, which made its nest beneath the naturalist's home on the Neuse River and roared in such a way that it shook the house and terrified the dog into silence. There was the Pos-sum, unique to America, which had such strength that, "if you break every Bone in their Skin, and mash their Skull, leaving them for Dead, you may come an hour after, and they will be gone quite away, or perhaps you meet them creeping away." When wolves are starving, Lawson said, they "go to a Swamp, and fill their Belly full of Mud." Of owls: "They often make Strangers lose their way in the woods." There were wonders in every direction, and he would report them, crafting a catalog of a whole new world.

The Indians would fare worse. Wave after wave of warfare and disease would follow, sweeping them away. Some tribes would not be noticed again and would enter eternity almost unrecognized on earth. Lawson's words of doom would come to pass: The greed and perfidy of white traders would cause catastrophe to the native inhabitants.

In 1712, Catesby would plunge into a different part of this wilderness. Further away in time and space, the Bartrams and Wilson and Audubon and other inquiring naturalists would find their way through unfamiliar landscape by foot, horseback, and canoe, carrying only what was essential to re-cord their findings. Pockets stuffed, each would come back with pieces of the truth—or counterfeits according to the truth. Feather by bright feather, the geography of American birds would be platted and described, at terrible cost to these adventurers, and not without unmistakable acts of plagiarism committed against the earlier itinerant naturalists.

Today the mosaic continues, expanded now to realms far overhead in space where insects, animals, and plants are launched, where spiders weave nevertheless, and ants colonize. Space probes bring back sounds of the universe, and some of these are like the songs of birds.

The astronomer William Herschel (1738-1822) referred to the sky as a garden. Stars, he said, germinate, bloom, fade, and wither as do plants; and, if we want to understand a certain type of heavenly body, we need to examine other members of its species, as we would in the plant world. Because Herschel carefully observed and noted the dynamism of the solar system, he was able to embark on its natural history. Because he did not try to disguise its chaos he was able to reveal its truth.

Vita Sackville-West planted a moon garden, all in white. Actually it was not only white but gray and green and what she said, as she planned it, is: "I cannot help hoping that the great ghostly barn owl will sweep silently across a pale garden, next summer, in the twilight—the pale garden that I am now planting, under the first flakes of snow."

Ghostly owls weave paths through a garden of stars while strangers lose their way in the woods: Such is the land between, and that land is everywhere.

One evening of the autumn equinox, I attended a ritual in a neighborhood park to celebrate the occasion. About thirty of us in growing dimness walked the park's labyrinth while chanting positive affirmations. The moon rose out of the woods beside us, when suddenly, and with no sound, a barn owl glided out of the trees, barely over our heads, and melted into the moonlight. Everything had been said, though we continued on with the chants, and even the drumming continued.

Naming and Seeing

My mother was gone and her apartment emptied out though not sold; the war in Iraq and other global worries had stalled real estate in New York. She was buried in the same grave with her fourth child, a son named Peter who died soon after birth. I arranged for both their names to be etched on the communal gravestone in the family plot. For some reason, Peter's name had never been added, nor did I know his middle name until I read the cemetery documents: Cantine, the name of my paternal grandmother, the one who lived in the 1812 house in Walpole and was buried in the village cemetery there. Undoubtedly, at the time, Peter's death was too painful to deal with. He could not be named in stone.

According to what I remember being told as a child, his death was the fault of the doctor, a well-known New York practitioner. When his birth was imminent, it was delayed until the doctor could get to the hospital. Peter Cantine died the day he was born because of complications related to the birth. My father never got over being sent a bill by the doctor. My mother told me this on two or three occasions. That is all I know of my small brother.

Until recently, I never understood what that terrible day of Peter's brief visit to earth must have been like. But in making funeral arrangements for my mother and studying the documents from Gate of Heaven Cemetery, I found its imprint (or at least that of the day he was buried): January 28, 1947. Another setting forth in January, and an incredibly arduous journey. Janus must have been asleep. Or rather, my Irish Catholic-French Huguenot Episcopal family would not think to pray to him and Peter slipped through, a tiny bird of passage. I was four years old and remember nothing of the event but came to know its weight. There were no pictures of Peter or any physical remnants to mark his quick visit to Earth. He was, simply, buried in silence.

Now, more than fifty years later, it is done, his name and his one day on earth etched in stone along with the inscriptions for my mother and her clan of McGuires, Cuddihys, and Gillespies. I try to imagine my brother alive today, not shadowy bones in a small box three levels deep under the bones of my beautiful Great Aunt Emma who was such a brilliant wit, and my mother, now resting on top.

What do I remember of this family gathering place that dares to name itself the Gate of Heaven? One windy August day as I visited, I saw a basket of flowers toppled and strewn near another grave, an arrangement ruined and left behind. This scene gripped my heart. *This* was the loneliest place on earth.

Later, another brother would be added to this mournful edifice, an older brother, again in a small box, this one of ashes, a brother who was estranged and lost to us all. Sheffield died at age 63 on February 7, 2005—another one setting off shadowed by violence in winter's depths.

After his funeral and burial at Gate of Heaven, family members and I returned to New York to walk Christo's and Jeanne-Claude's art project, "The Gates." This was a very different set of gates—huge orange-colored curtains placed throughout Central Park for a short exhibit. Twenty-three miles of the park's paths billowed with the bright display. With no message or particular purpose, this work of art was simply that—a work of art—which invited participation and new perspectives, in regard to both the park and one's self.

There is no way to explain it, but walking through the "Gates" with thousands of other people from all over the world changed us. The rolling parkscape softened; it was no longer a bare and bitter February. Some of the paralyzing agony lifted and we became lighter beings. If these gates did not lead to Heaven, at least they awoke our souls to its possibility.

Pain is a country that goes by many names and descriptions: column after column and all of it strange. Antoine de Saint-Exupéry said, "It's so mysterious, the land of tears." Its coastline is ragged and treacherous, filled with shoals and ever-shifting channels. It is easy to enter in and founder. It is hard, in this country, to make yourself understood by the inhabitants, all manifesting different experiences with different vocabulary and recording different field notes, following different guides and goals. They have no time for anyone else.

As you fumble to draft an accurate map, food will run out. Droughts and storms will persist. Savages will attack. Strange animals will follow you. Snakes, seeking warmth, will slither into your bed and lie against you as you sleep. You will encounter tortures no one wants to hear about or believe. To be flayed alive? To be set afire? To be crushed by stones? To be bitten by mosquitoes with horrible diseases? To have babies torn from the womb or left by doctors to strangle? To be marooned on an inhospitable island or a frozen shore while stars run away from the sky? Why do we come to such a place battered by fever, hurricane, treachery, and war? Some might say because lessons of past lives have not been learned; others because it is the course of history; others because we have not yet learned to love and this is the place we learn. And I would say because we are still searching for the true name of Love— we are still setting out on the river which moves this way and that and constantly divides. We are all John White, leading a group into historical disappearance or John Lawson pushing out into the unknown armed only with a notebook and pencil, and, if we're lucky, a spaniel at our side.

Relearning the Universe

We need to know how a Bobolink travels and why a meadowlark sings. We need to know the origin of the faces arising from the marshes: Do they come from our imagination or arrive in their own invisible and mysterious canoes? Are they from inside or outside? How does a Red-winged Blackbird build its grassy nest over water and learn its special song? What is the hiding place of memory? What happens to ours when we are gone and forgotten and what is remembered of us fades into oblivion?

Suddenly an egret rises and, distracted, I forget my mental struggles.

Sometimes, it is good to forget and simply to concentrate on the bird: What are its field marks, its song, its habitat, its shape? Can I name this bird?

I have come to know that *naming* the bird is not nearly so important as *seeing* the bird, recording the bird, and contemplating its image. Too much, especially among the self-serious, has been made of the power of naming, of assuming the role of Adam. Naming connotes ownership or, to use a more insidious term, "stewardship." Naming keeps order. Naming also determines point of view: The difference between the terms "pet" and "animal companion" is immense; and, as avian neuroscientists point out, how we name a bird's brain influences how we think about it; if we hold to old terminology we cannot change our thinking and move forward. We cannot take another fork in the river until we notice there is one.

If Herschel, the great observer, had not looked with his telescopes past the perceived stately order of the universe to the violence and disorder he detected, he would never have opened the door to the natural history of the heavens. If twentieth-century physicists had not looked into the subatomic world and found its random and fluid nature, we would still be frozen in a Newtonian construct. If astronomers did not persist, they would not have found Sedna, the frozen red world currently located at what we know to be the edge of space. And we continue to push beyond.

Relearning the universe can be difficult. In 2006, the International Astronomical Union (IAU) declassified Pluto as a planet. After vigorous debate concerning the definition for planets, Pluto was then reclassified as a "dwarf planet." It was not so much that Pluto, which had served as Earth's ninth planet since 1930, was being demoted, reclassifiers insisted; it was a matter of having learned more about heavenly bodies in general. There was no question of changing its name, "Pluto"—God of the Dead and Ruler of the Underworld—only a question of looking deeper into the Kuiper belt—that vast ring of other worlds where it resides—in order to establish a context. Now that the "New Horizons" spacecraft has flown by Pluto and its moons and returned remarkably clear photographs, we will re-analyze and perhaps reclassify once more our problematic ninth planet.

Likewise, we will learn more about Sedna, the coldest and most distant place known in the Solar System, and decide where to assign it in the taxonomy of space. We have been promised by astronomers, however, that the name—"Sedna"—will stay. What could be more appropriate than the Inuit goddess of the frozen seas? In the meantime, the Kepler spacecraft has discovered a planet outside our solar system that appears to be habitable. Other than Kepler 452b, what will it be called? And now there is also Proxima b, only 4.25 light-years away, which appears suitable for life and deserves an appropriate name. Today we recognize many more galaxies than originally thought. We count them by the billions. How can we not be lost in their endless hiding places? How vast can space be? And how can our limited language rise to the challenge of giving it names?

Lost Portraits

Eventually my mother's co-op apartment sold, and we heard it was to undergo extensive renovation. Now I can visit there only in memory. What do I see as I travel through those pictures in my mind?

In the foyer hangs a drawing of a woman with fan by Al Hirschfeld, who died at the age of 99 in January, 2003. He was known for hiding the name of his daughter Nina in the fluid lines of his theater caricatures: a puzzle for curious observers to solve.

As curator Amy R. W. Meyers points out, Catesby sometimes incorporated his signature into the image, such as making his initials appear to be the peeling-off of bark. Under these circumstances, subject, artist, and audience come together, each with a vital role. The artist wants us to be aware of his involvement with the subject; the audience wants to discover and make sense of what is presented. Physicists tell us the observer not only affects the observed but gives form to the observed: Until we watch, nothing happens.

But what happens when we stare into the painted eyes of an unidentified portrait, unable to name the subject or its maker and nothing comes back to us—no jolt of recognition?

My mother's walls also displayed a large painting of a woman who appeared to be a subject by Gainsborough, but no connection was ever proved, and the portrait of this mystery woman held her place in silence while we spun out our family drama just below her.

My mother's beautiful younger sister Emma, whom we knew as Aime, savior of the injured swan—this sister was in love, I remember being told as a child, with a man whose name I recall as Bunny Lawson. I think they were engaged, or close to it. Then he disappeared from his sailboat in the Atlantic Ocean, in the "Bermuda Triangle," it was said. His undisturbed boat was found, but no trace of him. Aime came to be the guardian of a full-size portrait of Lawson's mother as a child. Late in life, Aime married a man named JoZach, who came from Kansas and had large holdings in Texas. While they were living in Oyster Bay, close to my family's house, Aime died. JoZach had her buried in Texas, in his family mausoleum in Belton, near Waco. I remember standing by the coffin as the priest, his robe fluttering in a warm wind, told us there is nothing so important but that we love one another.

Years later, we visited JoZach, who had since remarried, at his new home in Sarasota, Florida. Soon after they married, Jo-Zach's second wife succumbed to Alzheimer's. We never met her.

We went to visit him, several times. Hanging on his dining room wall, behind his chair, was the life-size portrait of Bunny Lawson's mother as a child, an orphan painting. I knew there was no one else besides us, anywhere on earth, who was familiar with the story or the provenance of the portrait. How far had the painted image of this child drifted from everything that was home to it? And who would even know when there was no one left with any connection to it?

When JoZach died, I considered giving the portrait a home, but his family, fearing we were gold-diggers, would not communicate with us, and so, Bunny Lawson's mother floated away, along with a bust of Aime and other belongings of hers which would have little or no meaning to anyone else. Also, there was a set of gilt-edged blue willoware dinner plates that was meant to go to me.

Yes, these are only things, but what a terrible loneliness has grown around them, flotsam wandering the earth like small phantom ships sailing ancient maps towards nonexistent ports. Where will they turn up next? Who will wonder of their history and have a kindly thought for them? Who will put fork to Blue Willow plate and think of my beautiful aunt, her body lying in a vault scoured by the Texas wind and know that her mother—my grandmother—gave those plates to her as a wedding present?

It is not unusual for portraits to become unanchored and shipwrecked on the shoals of time, but this one stays in my mind. My Aunt Aime was so kind, her story so sad, and this little girl in the painting so innocent, a victim of missed connections and lost communications who might have stepped out of a Thomas Hardy novel.

Bunny Lawson disappeared, and now I am the only one who knows. He has thus disappeared twice, once from his sailboat and once from those who knew of him—that little colony on a fragile shore. If we were to go back to try to find that colony, we would be disappointed: its traces will soon be lost, leaving behind perhaps a few shards and some feathers—and maybe a word like Croatoan scratched in haste into a tree trunk.

When you live to be the oldest in your family—the sparrow on the rooftop—how do you keep all these memories together and how do you bequeath them to someone else who has no awareness of them, or perhaps no interest?

Or does any of it matter? Should we try to preserve a name if a name is all that is left? And is this really our responsibility? When you go to cleaning out closets, boxes, and files, you have to ask. I remember my twelve-year-old grandson declaring that nothing that happens on earth affects anything in the universe. I want to argue with him. I want to believe something matters, something as small as our individual lives.

Remember, "there is no trash bird": each bird matters. Remember the endless flocks flying before you to bring you to this place. For the most part they were blackbirds, indistinguishable but determined. They got us here; that has to matter.

I think my guides would advise this: Just do your work and have no concerns about the consequences. Look closely at the bird and make careful notes. Focus.

Blackbird Flying

It is just ten years since I traveled from the West Indies to New York in a March blizzard to visit my mother, whose memory was beginning to fail, and to find original copies of Marian's *Metamorphosis*. Since, I have gone back to the Carolina coast over and over. I know the plane routes and schedules, the weather, and some of what to expect when I look out over my watery vista. But every time I look, there is more.

I think of that night Tim, our young friend, walked through closed doors to visit us as he was dying several miles away. Walls, he taught, are permeable; love and longing have no barriers. Change is everything. If only I could have called out, "Wait, Tim! Tell me where you are going."

Herschel was right—destruction is necessary. The marsh is a garden as the sky is a garden, germinating, blooming, fading, and withering—and always growing out towards the sea. Voyages of discovery grow there, too, releasing images like seed pods over the wavering coastline. If you look, you see blackbird flying, weaving in and out of the grass as it forages for grain and insects. If you look carefully—just beyond the flash of wings—you will see that *there* is the binding of earth and heaven; *there* is the beginning of the natural history of Love. It has no name. Perhaps it never will.

Bibliography

Catesby, Mark. *Catesby's Birds of Colonial America*, ed. by Alan Feduccia. Chapel Hill: The University of North Carolina Press, 1985.

Elliott, William. *Carolina Sports by Land and Water.* Columbia: The University of South Carolina Press, 1994.

Lawson, John. *A New Voyage to Carolina*, ed. by Hugh Talmage Lefler. Chapel Hill: The University of North Carolina Press, 1967.

McCartney, Paul. www.beatlesbooks.com/blackbird.

Merian, Maria Sibylla. *Metamorphosis Insectorum Surinamensium.* First edition, 1705.

Milton, Giles. *Big Chief Elizabeth.* New York: Macmillan Publishers, 2000.

Rhyne, Nancy. *Voices of Carolina Slave Children.* Orangeburg, South Carolina: Sandlapper Publishing, 1999.

Rothenberg, David. *Why Birds Sing.* New York: Basic Books, 2005.

Sibley, David Allen. *The Sibley Guide to Bird Life & Behavior.* New York: Alfred A. Knopf, Inc., 2001.

The Sibley Field Guide to Birds of Eastern North America. New York: Alfred A. Knopf, Inc., 2003.

CPSIA information can be obtained
at www.ICGtesting.com
Printed in the USA
FSHW012147100219
55597FS

9 780999 808962